President Abraham
Lincoln

General William T.
Sherman

President Jefferson
Davis

and the
Lost
Confederate
Gold

Patricia G. McNeely

Lincoln, Sherman, Davis and the Lost Confederate Gold

1st edition

Copyright © 2015 Patricia G. McNeely

ISBN-13: 978-1517212384

ISBN-10: 1517212383

Printed in the United States of America

United States—History—Civil war, 1861-1865—President Abraham Lincoln—General William T. Sherman—President Jefferson Davis—John Wilkes Booth—Assassination—Confederate Gold

Cover design by Sharon Kelly
Cover photograph of gold chest by Patricia G. McNeely
Images of Lincoln, Sherman, Davis: Library of Congress

For additional information or to arrange for book readings or presentations, contact the author at McNeely2000@gmail.com

DEDICATED

TO

ALICE WOODSON
AND WILLIAM A. GANTT SR.

AND

AL, ALLISON, ALAN
JORDAN AND JULIA
MCNEELY

OTHER BOOKS BY PATRICIA G. MCNEELY

 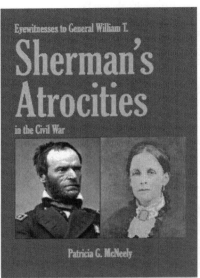

SHERMAN'S FLAME AND BLAME CAMPAIGN THROUGH GEORGIA AND THE CAROLINAS ... AND THE BURNING OF COLUMBIA

EYEWITNESSES TO GENERAL SHERMAN'S ATROCITIES IN THE CIVIL WAR

KNIGHTS OF THE QUILL: CONFEDERATE CORREPONDENTS AND THEIR CIVIL WAR REPORTING

FIGHTING WORDS: A MEDIA HISTORY OF SOUTH CAROLINA

PALMETTO PRESS: THE HISTORY OF SOUTH CAROLINA NEWSPAPERS

HANDWRITTEN RECIPES AND MEMORIES FROM AMERICA'S FIRST FAMILIES

ACKNOWLEDGEMENTS

I owe everlasting thanks to dozens of friends and colleagues for their assistance and support. I'm singling out those who have spent the most time and effort helping me along the way, even though many others have helped in small ways and big. For all of them, I am eternally grateful.

My husband, Al, drove me to dozens of Civil War sites with (almost) no complaining, and ate a lot of take-out meals, and our children Allison and Alan were always interested and encouraging.

My most heartfelt gratitude goes to Sharon Kelly, who spent countless hours helping me cope with never-ending formatting problems and designed the cover on this book.

Dr. Henry T. Price is always a significant life-saver who spent days editing my book. I am always grateful for his help.

Doug Fisher is on call 24-hours a day for my endless questions and spent a week out of his life this summer recording "Sherman's Flame and Blame Campaign through Georgia and the Carolinas... and the Burning of Columbia" for the S.C. State Library's Talking Books for the Blind.

Henry H. "Hank" Schulte did last minute copyediting and was an almost daily source of inspiration and support. His daughter Margaret Schulte was always encouraging and sent "happy spots" to help me along the way.

Debbie Bloom and the Walker Local History Room at the Richland Library are amazing resources. Debbie has been my constant source of help in finding obscure and out-of-print publications and documents.

Steve White spent hours hunting for information and leading us on tours wherever we needed to go, and he always shows up to help.

Bill Rogers and Jen Madden at the S. C. Press Association are a never-ending source of help and inspiration, and Jay Bender and Carmen Maye, who are lawyers and professors at the University of South Carolina, are a fount of legal information.

The South Caroliniana staff at the University of South Carolina is amazing. I'm always grateful to Allen Stokes, the retired director, and Henry Fulmer, the current director, as well as Brian Cuthrell and Graham Duncan Beth Bilderback coordinated the images quickly and efficiently.

Elizabeth Suddeth and Jeffrey Mahala in the Irvin Department of Rare Books and Special Collections in the Ernest F. Hollings Special Collections Library at the University of South Carolina are always significant resources.

And I must always thank Dr. David Sachsman, who holds the George R. West Chair of Excellence at the University of Tennessee in Chattanooga and is director of the annual Symposium on the 19th Century Press, the Civil War and Free Expression. He and his symposium are always an inspiration.

TABLE OF CONTENTS

INTRODUCTION

When I finished my last Civil War book about "Sherman's Flame and Blame Campaign through Georgia and the Carolinas," I was intrigued by the Johnson administration's public implications that General Sherman had accepted a bribe of up to $13 million in Confederate gold to let President Davis escape through North Carolina.

I disregarded that until I found an article in a 1913 Newberry, S.C., newspaper in which Jim Jones, who was President Davis' free servant, said he was sent from Richmond to Newberry in early March 1865 with chests containing $13 million in gold and English notes.

Instead of denying that he had accepted a bribe, Sherman was "angry about the tone and substance" of the published bulletins. That information, along with the fact that Sherman, Jones and General Henry Halleck mentioned the same amounts of Confederate gold, set me off on an historical treasure hunt of my own.

The results were amazing. I found loose threads of history that bound together the destinies of General Sherman, Jefferson Davis and President Lincoln with the Lost Confederate Gold. Before his assassination, Lincoln had made it clear to his cabinet and Sherman that he wanted the Confederate leaders to quietly and unofficially "escape the country" when the war was over. Regardless of whether Sherman was bribed or just remembering Lincoln's last wishes, Sherman allowed Davis and his cabinet to ride openly through North Carolina within touching distance of Federal armies. Defending his actions, Sherman said in his memoirs that he did not know he was supposed to capture the Confederate president.

After officially implying that Sherman had accepted a bribe and let Davis escape, Halleck issued orders to Sherman's subordinate generals to "obey no orders from Sherman" and notified all commanders on the Mississippi "to take measures to intercept the rebel chiefs and their plunder" who were known to be headed for the Trans-Mississippi region to continue the war.

Soon after the official Federal chase began, President Johnson issued a $100,000 reward for the capture of the Confederate president because the administration was claiming Davis had been involved in the conspiracy to assassinate Lincoln. The rewards also included Jacob Thompson and Clement C. Clay, who had briefly been secret agents in Canada trying to lure Federal armies to the northern borders at the end of 1864. The activities of the secret agents in Canada also intrigued me, and I found more loose threads of history wrapped around the Lincoln assassination conspiracy.

Another loose thread was a startling story involving a man who died in 1893 in Enid, Oklahoma, who had convincing information that he was John Wilkes Booth and that a man named "Ruggles" had died in his place in Garrett's barn. Descendants are now trying to gain access to three vertebrae taken in the Booth autopsy to compare DNA with his brother Edwin Booth. The descendants want to know if the body brought back from the barn to Washington, D.C., was really the body of the famous actor.

As for the Lost Confederate Gold, I found that the most famous treasure—the well-documented $950,000 in treasury and bank gold that left Richmond—was just a fraction of the civilian gold and other valuables in the Confederacy that were stolen, hidden or disappeared before the Federal government launched an international hunt through the Confederacy and England in search of any gold and other money that had been overlooked.

I've also tracked down images of people and events so that we can really visualize what happened in those last amazing days at the end of the Civil War.

Pat McNeely   October 2015

1 THE ASSASSINATION CONSPIRACIES BEGIN

Conspiracies to kidnap or assassinate Abraham Lincoln began soon after his election in November 1860 and continued until he was murdered at the end of the Civil War.

Abraham Lincoln in 1865
Source: Library of Congress

As early as February 23, 1861, Intelligence Service Agent Allan Pinkerton was convinced that Lincoln would be ambushed in Baltimore on the way to his inauguration in Washington, D.C. To thwart the attack, Lincoln agreed to travel on an earlier special train, and by the time the crowd gathered to see the President-elect on his scheduled stop, he had already passed through Baltimore in a sleeping car.[1]

Harper's Weekly, March 6, 1861

Although Lincoln believed it was a serious assassination threat, newspapers treated the episode with ridicule and erupted with humiliating stories and cartoons about his secret flight.[2] Newspapers of all parties lampooned Lincoln. Images like the ones in *Harper's Weekly* of the President fleeing in a Scotch-plaid cap and long military cloak plagued Lincoln throughout his presidency as enemies and newspapers rehashed the story of his secret trip through Baltimore.[3]

Lincoln quickly regretted the midnight ride and frequently upbraided his old friend and escort Ward Hill Lamon for helping him "degrade himself" at a time when he thought his behavior should have "exhibited the utmost dignity and composure."[4]

Ward Hill Lamon
Source: Library of Congress

Lamon, who was his former law partner, said, "Neither he nor the country generally then understood the true facts concerning the dangers to his life."[5]

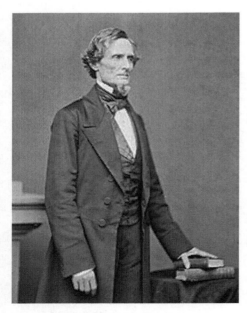

President Jefferson Davis
Source: Library of Congress

Reluctantly in August 1862, President Lincoln told Lamon about an attempt on his life that almost succeeded.[6]

Lincoln had ridden alone on the three-mile trip from the White House to the Soldiers Home on Old Abe, a horse he delighted in riding. As he jogged along at a slow gait, he was deep in thought about what would happen next in the unsettled state of affairs.[7]

When he arrived at the foot of the hill on the

road leading to the entrance of the Home grounds, he was suddenly aroused. "I may say the arousement lifted me out of my saddle as well as out of my wits by the report of a rifle and seemingly the gunner was not fifty yards from where my contemplations ended and my accelerated transit began," Lincoln said.[8]

"My erratic namesake with little warning gave proof of decided dissatisfaction at the racket and with one reckless bound, he unceremoniously separated me from my eight dollar plug hat with which I parted company without any assent expressed or implied upon my part."[9]

Riding at break-neck speed, Lincoln arrived in a haven of safety. "Meanwhile I was left in doubt whether death was more desirable from being thrown from a runaway federal horse or as the tragic result of a rifle ball fired by a disloyal bushwhacker in the middle of the night."[10]

Except for telling his friend Lamon about the incident, Lincoln insisted on keeping the encounter a secret, saying that "no good can result at this time from giving it publicity."[11]

Old Soldiers Home in Washington, D.C. *Source: Library of Congress*

General Judson Kilpatrick
Source: Library of Congress

Lamon, who helped provide protection for Lincoln, was horrified, and his warnings about Lincoln's safety escalated. However, Lincoln was unconcerned.

"It does seem to me that I am in more danger from the augmentation of imaginary peril than from a judicious silence, be the danger ever so great," Lincoln said, "and, moreover, I do not want it understood that I share your apprehensions. I never have."[12]

As the war progressed, an effort was also made to assassinate President Jefferson Davis. The plot developed after Lincoln wrote to General Joseph Hooker [13] on May 8, 1863,[14] saying that he had just met with General August Willich, whom the Confederates had released from Libby Prison in Richmond. "[Willich] was there when our cavalry cut the roads in that vicinity," Lincoln wrote. "He says there was not a sound pair [of] legs in Richmond, and that our men, had they known it, could have safely gone in and burnt everything & brought us Jeff. Davis."[15]

Lincoln's suggestion was converted into action on February 28, 1864, when General H. Judson Kilpatrick led a column of 3,584 troopers with sabers across the Rapidan River toward Richmond. Ostensibly to free the federal prisoners of war in Libby Prison and nearby Belle Isle camp, Kilpatrick actually had orders to assassinate Davis and his cabinet and to burn Richmond.[16]

While Kilpatrick tried to enter the city and divert the Confederates with his large force of cavalry, 21-year-old

Colonel Ulric Dahlgren led a supporting column of 500 men on the opposite side of town to within 2 ½ miles of the heart of the city in an effort to carry out the mission. Dahlgren's men had combustible material with which they planned to destroy the city, according to Confederate Captain John W. Headley.[17]

"It appears that General Kilpatrick and Colonel Dahlgren came directly from a conference in Washington with President Lincoln and acted by his authority and approval, just as the army commanders were doing who were burning the homes and property of the citizens of the South," Headley said.[18]

Kilpatrick's forces were driven back, and Dahlgren was killed in the raid, but Confederates found papers on his body labeled "Special Orders and Instructions" that said in part, "The men must be kept together and well in

Lieutenant Ulric Dahlgren (standing) with some of his soldiers.
Source: Library of Congress

hand, and once in the city, it must be destroyed and Jeff Davis and his cabinet killed."[19]

The papers were forwarded through military and political chains of command and ultimately to Davis. When the contents were published, calls for retribution and retaliation rippled across the South, Headley said, but the Lincoln administration denied any assassination plans and declared the documents to be forgeries.[20]

The ten Federals captured in the raid were sent to Libby Prison where they were threatened with executions that were never carried out. Dahlgren's body, which had been dumped in a muddy grave near the place he fell, was disinterred and put on display in Richmond. [21]

After the assassination attempt on his life, Davis decided to widen Confederate espionage operations by sending secret agents to Canada on May 30, 1864, to begin hostile movements in the U.S. northern territory.[22]

Jacob Thompson
Source: Library of Congress

Jefferson selected Jacob Thompson of Oxford, Mississippi, for the six-month assignment. One of the wealthiest men in the South, he was a lawyer and statesman who had served in Congress and as Secretary of the Interior in the cabinet of President James Buchanan.[23]

Thompson was joined by Senator Clement C. Clay, Jr., an Alabama lawyer who resigned from the Confederate Congress to help organize the Department of the North.

For their first espionage activities operated out of Toronto, the agents supported a northern group known as Sons of Liberty in what was hoped would be a general uprising to detach Illinois, Indiana, Ohio and Kentucky from the Union by overthrowing their governments to • form a Northwestern Confederacy.[24] Clement Vallandigham was a U.S Representative for two terms before the Civil War. He became the acknowledged leader of the Copperheads, who were Democrats in northern states who opposed the war. In an

Clement C. Clay
Source: Library of Congress

address on May 8, 1862, he coined their slogan, "To maintain the Constitution as it is, and to restore the Union as it was."

Clement Vallandigham
Source: Library of Congress

While in Canada, Vallandigham met with Jacob Thompson to discuss plans to form the Northwestern Confederacy and to ask for money and military support for an uprising during November 1864. The uprising never materialized because the Confederates could not supply enough military support.[25] The plan also included an attempt to capture[26] the *U.S.S. Michigan* and release Confederate prisoners on Johnson's Island, Ohio,[27] but that failed and Captain John Yates Beall was captured and executed.

John Yates Beall
Source: Library of Congress

Confederate agents did succeed in robbing $200,000 from banks in St. Albans, Vermont, on Lake Champlain on October 19, 1864.[28]

The robberies were retaliation for all the atrocities against civilians committed by Federal soldiers in the South[29] and to try to force the Union Army to divert troops to defend their northern border.[30]

The agents in Canada supported a scheme to devalue the currency in New York by exchanging paper money for gold. They had succeeded in exchanging $2 million when one of the agents was arrested and the plan was abandoned.[31] However, the gold wasn't transported back into the Richmond treasury. And on May 28, 2015, USA TODAY reported that treasure hunters believe they may have found $2 million in gold in a Lake Michigan shipwreck. They believe the treasure was stolen from the Confederates after the Civil War.[32]

Agents also supported efforts to disrupt the November 8, 1864, presidential election in New York for Lincoln's second term, but those plans were thwarted by an infusion of federal troops.[33]   Enraged by the Union

Army's scorched earth campaign against Southern military installations and industrial sites but most of all, civilian property, the agents tried to set fire to New York City, but that effort failed because their plan had been reported to the Federals by a mole who had provided defective Greek fire bombs (fire in bottles).[34]

The U.S.S. Michigan was renamed Wolverine after the war.
Source: Library of Congress

All of the Confederate plots devised by the Secret Service in Canada, except for the St. Albans robberies, had been doomed to failure from the start because of the treachery of Godfrey J. Hyams of Little Rock, Arkansas. He

was a Federal spy in their offices in Toronto and had given U.S. detectives information about all the leading Confederates who operated on the border.[35]

After the series of massive failures and only one success, the Canadian office closed in January 1865, but two agents making their way back into the Confederacy were in St. Louis on February 24 when Vice President-Elect

Vice President Andrew Johnson
Source: Library of Congress

Andrew Johnson was staying at the Louisville Hotel. On the spur of the moment, the agents decided to kidnap Johnson and exchange him for Beall, or carry him to Virginia as a prisoner of war.[36]

Their quick but elaborate plans failed when Johnson left town on an early morning boat.[37]

2 JOHN WILKES BOOTH HUNTS FOR COLLABORATORS

Handsome, dark-haired, 27-year-old John Wilkes Booth was one of the most popular and successful actors in America in 1865, usually averaging about $290,000 a year in today's dollars.[38] An illegitimate son of English Shakespearian actor Junius Brutus Booth, he was popular in social circles and secretly engaged to Lucy Lambert Hale, the daughter of New Hampshire Senator John P. Hale.[39] A devout Confederate and anti-

John Wilkes Booth
Source: Library of Congress

George A. Townsend
New York World reporter
Source: Library of Congress

abolitionist, Booth began hatching plans in mid-1863 to capture President Abraham Lincoln and take him to Richmond.[40]

Booth's motives were clear, and he openly admitted that he was willing to die in the effort: "My love (as things stand today) is for the South alone," he said. "Nor do I deem it a dishonor in attempting to make for her a prisoner of this man (Lincoln) to whom she owes so much of misery....I will proudly beg permission to triumph or die in that same 'ditch' by her side."[41]

Although Booth's name was not on any of the lists of operatives associated with the Canadian operations, Booth apparently sought help in Canada from Confederate agents Thompson, Clay, Larry McDonald and others who, according to *New York World* reporter George Alfred Townsend, "were

Booth's fiancé, Lucy Lambert Hale
Source: Library of Congress

involved in enough espionage and intrigue that Booth felt he had but to seek an interview with them."[42]

While Booth was fine-tuning his plans to kidnap Lincoln, he visited Canada "at least once and probably three times, it is believed, stopping once in Montreal at St. Lawrence Hall and banking $455 at the Ontario bank," according to Townsend. That was not espionage money, but "his own money," Townsend said. "I have myself seen his bankbook with the single entry of this amount."

Townsend said Booth's bankbook was found in Kirkwood's Hotel in a room rented by George Atzerodt, a house painter, blockade runner and mail carrier across the Potomac who would be hanged for his role in the conspiracy.[43] Atzerodt said he became involved at the end of February 1865 when Booth and Surratt wanted a man who understood boating and could get a boat and ferry a

George Atzerodt Source: Library of Congress

party over the Potomac. Surratt knew him and "under promises of a fortune," Atzerodt agreed to furnish the boat and do the ferrying.[44]

Vice President Andrew Johnson was also staying at Kirkwood's Hotel on the night of the assassination, and it was the place where Johnson was sworn into office as President at 11 a.m. on April 15.[45]

Townsend was positive that although the Canadian agents knew Booth and "patted his back, calling him, like Macbeth, the prince of cut throats, I am equally certain that Booth's project was unknown in Richmond. No word nor written line, no clue of any sort has been found attaching Booth to the confederate authorities."[46]

And, if these agents entertained Booth's suggestion at all, Townsend said, "they plainly told him that he carried his life in his dagger's edge and could expect from them neither aid nor exculpation.[47]

The Surratt House. Source: Library of Congress

"If Booth received no positive instructions, he was at any rate adjudged a man likely to be of use and therefore introduced to the rebel agencies in and around Washington," Townsend said.

"Doubtless by direct letter or verbal instruction he received a password to the house of Mrs. (Mary) Surratt,"[48] who managed a tavern in Surrattsville, Maryland, and was hanged after Lincoln's assassination. There, Booth met her son John, who Townsend said was a "spy in the secret service of the Southern Confederacy, plying his service between Richmond, Virginia, Washington, D.C., New York City and Montreal, Canada."[49]

By 1864, efforts to kidnap or assassinate Lincoln had increased so much from multiple directions that his old friend Ward Hill Lamon sent him a strident, urgent warning on December 10, saying, "You are in danger.

Tonight as you have done on several previous occasions you went unattended to the theatre. When I say unattended I mean that you went alone with Charles Sumner and a foreign minister, neither of whom could defend himself against an assault from any able bodied woman in this city."[50]

Lamon urgently warned Lincoln that he ought to know that his life was sought after and would be taken unless he and his friends were cautious, "for you have many enemies within our lines. You certainly know that I have provided men at your mansion to perform all necessary police duty, and I am always ready myself to perform any duty that will properly conduce to your interest or your safety."[51]

Although not originally part of the conspiracy, Thomas A. Jones, who would play the most significant role in Booth's escape after the assassination, had taken a job in 1862 as the chief signal agent north of the Potomac in charge of Confederate mail and the boats along the river.[52] Jones was chosen for that job primarily because of the location of his dark, rain-washed

JOHN H. SURRATT.
IN HIS CANADA JACKET,

John Surratt in his Canada uniform
Source: Library of Congress

one-story house located on a 540-acre farm near Port Tobacco, Maryland.[53] His land was bounded on the west by the Potomac River and on the north by Pope's Creek, a 50-foot-wide waterway that was sixty miles from Washington, D.C., by water and forty miles by land; so his farm was in the best location for easy access between Maryland and Virginia.[54]

The 45-year-old "thin and mournful looking" mail agent was unaware of Booth's plots and had never met the actor or any of the conspirators before the attacks in Washington on April 14, 1865. Not until December 1864 did Jones first hear rumors about a "big scheme" to abduct Lincoln in Washington and take him prisoner.[55]

"Briefly stated, the plan was this," Jones said. "The President, when he went for his

Thomas A. Jones Source: Library of Congress

customary evening drive toward the Navy Yard, was to be seized and either chloroformed or gagged, and driven quietly out of the city. If in crossing the Navy Yard bridge the carriage should be stopped, the captors would point to the President and drive on. The carriage was to be escorted out of the city by men dressed in Federal uniform. Relays of fast horses were in readiness all along the route, and a boat in which to take the captive across the Potomac was kept on the west side of Port Tobacco Creek, about three and a half miles from the town of the same name."[56]

Jones said there was not much danger that the carriage containing the abducted President would be overtaken because the pursuers would be unable to obtain fresh horses.[57]

Louis J. Weichman
Source: Library of Congress

"The distance to be traversed to reach the Potomac was only about thirty miles, and with the boat and men to row it in readiness, the river could be crossed within an hour of the time it was reached," he said.[58]

"The idea of the conspirators was that with such a hostage in its power the Confederacy would be able to dictate terms to the North," Jones said.[59] Although Jones was not originally part of the conspiracy, he liked the rumors he had heard.

Louis J. Weichman, who was one of the chief witnesses for the prosecution at the assassination trial, said the gang of working conspirators tried a similar scheme in early March 1865 when three of them left on horseback for the vicinity of the Soldiers' Home in Washington "to capture President Lincoln and deliver him to the rebel authorities."[60]

Weichman said, "The gang, including John Wilkes

Booth, (Lewis) Payne and John Surratt, rode out on horseback one afternoon" a few days before Lincoln's inauguration on March 4 "and returned very much excited and discomposed, as if baffled in some cherished undertaking. The supposition was that an attempt to waylay the President at that time was really attempted and miscarried."[61]

Although Weichman had cooperated and knew their purpose, he was skeptical later about what had really happened that day.[62]

"The scheme to carry off Mr. Lincoln in broad daylight, to the Confederate lines, was too absurdly impracticable to have been really entertained by Booth, at least, if any of his fellow conspirators were crackbrained enough to be deluded by it," said Weichman, who was also skeptical about Booth's real intentions in stalking the President.

"There is little doubt that Booth meant murder whenever he should come in contact with the President and be able to deal the blow with any chance of escape."[63]

Whatever his goal, Booth didn't think any of his plans were "absurdly impracticable," including the one that followed a few days later on March 4, when he attended Lincoln's second inauguration and scuffled with a policeman in an effort to get to the inaugural platform.

Robert Strong, who was a policeman at the Capitol on the day of Lincoln's inauguration, was stationed at the east door of the rotunda when the President and others passed out to the platform where the ceremonies were about to begin.

Strong said suddenly a man in a "very determined and excited manner" broke through the line of policemen formed to keep the crowd out. "Lieutenant (J.W.) Westfall immediately seized the stranger and a considerable

President Lincoln's second inauguration in Washington, D.C.
Source: Library of Congress

scuffle ensued," Strong said. "The stranger seemed determined to get to the platform where the President and his party were but Lieutenant Westfall called for assistance."[64]

Commissioner B.B. French closed the door, and the intruder was pushed out of the passage leading to the platform reserved for the President's party. Six weeks later after the President was assassinated, policemen who were at the inauguration were still talking about the stranger's conduct.[65]

"Lieutenant Westfall procured a photograph of the assassin Booth soon after the death of the President and (without identification) showed it to Commissioner French in my presence and in the presence of several other policemen and asked him if he had ever met that man," Strong said. "The commissioner examined it attentively and said, 'Yes, I would know that face among ten thousand. That is the man you had a scuffle with on inauguration day. That is the same man.'"[66]

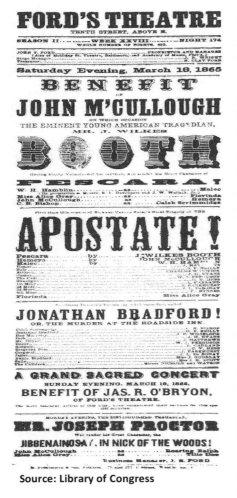

After another officer said he also recognized the photograph, Lieutenant Westfall said, "This is the picture of J. Wilkes Booth. Major French exclaimed, 'My God, what a fearful risk we ran that day.'"[67]

Although Booth's efforts to kidnap Lincoln continued to fail, they increased in frequency, and the conspiracy plots were expanded to include attacks on Secretary of State William H. Seward, Vice President Andrew Johnson, and other members of the cabinet.[68]

While Booth was fine-turning his conspireacies and planning the greatest theatrical role he would ever play, he continued as one of America's most popular and well-known actors, playing Romeo to Avonia Jones's Juliet at the National Theater while rehearsing at the Ford Theater for "Pescara, the Apostate," which was opening in March.[69]

3 GENERAL SHERMAN ENDS HIS CAMPAIGN

While John Wilkes Booth was plotting to kidnap President Lincoln, General William T. Sherman was nearing the end of his destructive campaign through Georgia and the Carolinas.

When Sherman reached Fayetteville, North Carolina on March 12, he sent a letter to Secretary of War Edwin Stanton

General William T. Sherman
Source: Library of Congress

saying that Charleston and Georgetown, South Carolina, and Wilmington, North Carolina, "are incidents, while the utter demolition of the railroad system of South Carolina, and the utter destruction of the enemy's arsenals of Columbia, Cheraw and Fayetteville, are the principals of the movement. These points were regarded as in-accessible to us, and now no place in the Confederacy is against the army of the West. Let Lee hold on to Richmond, and we will destroy his country; and then of what use is Richmond. He must come out and fight us on open ground, and for that we must ever be ready. Let him stick behind his parapets, and he will perish."[70]

He said that at Columbia and Cheraw, "we destroyed nearly all the gunpowder and cartridges which the Confederacy had in this part of the country."[71]

When Sherman corresponded with Grant, he said, "Our march, was substantially what I designed—straight on Columbia, feigning (sic) on Branchville and Augusta. We destroyed, in passing, the railroad from the Edisto nearly up to Aiken; again, from Orangeburg to the Congaree; again from Columbia down to Kingsville on the Wateree, and up toward Charlotte as far as the Chester line; thence we turned east on Cheraw and Fayetteville. At Columbia we destroyed immense arsenals and railroad establishments, among which were forty-three cannon. At Cheraw we found also machinery and material of war sent from Charleston, among which were twenty-five guns and thirty-six hundred barrels of powder; and here we find about twenty guns and a magnificent United States' arsenal."[72]

Continuing his strategy of destroying instead of occupying cities in his path, Sherman said he had not left detachments, and he planned to destroy the arsenal in Fayetteville so the enemy would not have its use. "And the United States should never again confide such valuable property to a people who have betrayed a trust," he said.[73] He said the railroad from Charlotte to Danville was all that was left but those would soon be destroyed.

In his destructive campaign through Georgia and the Carolinas, Sherman had made full use of an act passed by the U.S. Congress on July 17, 1862, that authorized the confiscation and sale of Confederate property and had given the military extraordinary powers to confiscate and destroy Confederate property. The Federals were authorized to claim three classes of property: "(1) 'captured' property or anything seized by the army and navy; (2) "abandoned" property, the owner being in the Confederate service, no matter whether his family were present or not; and (3) 'confiscable' property, or that liable to seizure and sale under the Confiscation Act of July 17, 1862."[74]

General Alfred H. Terry
Source: Library of Congress

Sherman had used those acts most effectively in his devastating war on civilian property in his campaign through Georgia and the Carolinas and the burning of Columbia, South Carolina.

The U.S. Supreme Court had ruled on March 12, 1863, that "disloyal" owners might become "loyal" by pardon and thus have all rights of property restored. "This was the effect of proclamations of the President (Lincoln). The restoration of the proceeds (then) became the absolute right of persons pardoned."[75] However, General Orders 120 that Sherman issued in Atlanta provided that foragers were to leave no receipts for confiscated, stolen and destroyed property, and he arranged for identification to be removed from cotton and other confiscated goods being shipped out of Savannah so that no claims could be made against the Federal government after the war.

Pleased with the destruction of the South Carolina supply lines to General Lee, Sherman wrote to Major General Alfred Howe Terry, commanding U.S. Forces in Wilmington, saying, "The people of South Carolina, instead of feeding Lee's army, will now call on Lee to feed them."[76] Sherman knew that Lee's supply lines had been further hampered by Sheridan's destructive cavalry raids in the Shenandoah Valley, and he could barely feed his own army.

As the starving and homeless people who were left in Sherman's wake struggled to find food and shelter,

Sherman turned his attention to getting rid of as many as 30,000 freedmen and other refugees who had followed his army into Fayetteville. Sherman wanted to leave Fayetteville immediately, but he could not because he "wanted to clear my columns of the vast crowd of refugees and negroes that encumber us. Some I will send down the river in boats, and the rest to Wilmington by land, under small escort, as soon as we are across Cape Fear River.[77] I must rid our army of from twenty to thirty thousand useless mouths; as many to go down Cape Fear (river) as possible, and the rest to go in vehicles or on captured horses via Clinton to Wilmington."[78]

General Oliver Howard reported to Sherman that he had secured one of the Confederate steamboats below Fayetteville, and General Henry Slocum was securing two more known to be above the city. "We will load them with refugees (white and black) who have clung to our skirts, impeded our movements, and consumed our food."[79]

In a letter to Terry, Sherman said, "We have swept the country well from Savannah to here, and the men and

Starving and homeless refugees moved into Federal lines at the end of the Civil War. Source: Library of Congress

animals are in fine condition. Had it not been for the foul weather, I would have caught Hardee at Cheraw or here (Fayetteville); but at Columbia, Cheraw, and here, we have captured immense stores, and destroyed machinery, guns, ammunition, and property, of inestimable value to our enemy. At all points he has fled from us."[80]

Sherman said that General Joseph Johnston might try to interpose between his troops in Fayetteville and Scho-

General Joseph Johnston
Source: Library of Congress

field about Newbern, but finally decided that Johnston would probably concentrate his scattered armies at Raleigh, and "I will go straight at him as soon as I get our men reclothed and our wagons reloaded." He asked General Grant to "keep everybody busy, and let (General George) Stoneman push toward Greensboro or Charlotte from Knoxville; even a feint in that quarter will be most important."[81]

In the meantime, Sherman said, "I had dispatched by land to Wilmington a train of refugees who had followed the army all the way from Columbia, South Carolina, under an escort of two hundred men...so that we were disencumbered, and prepared for instant battle on our left and exposed flank."[82]

Thus unencumbered, Sherman's army crossed Cape Fear River on March 15 on the march toward Goldsboro and was thirteen miles out on the Raleigh road when it skirmished briefly with General William J. Hardee's infantry, artillery and cavalry. Hardee had taken up a strong position at Averasboro, North Carolina, but by the next morning, he was retreating toward Smithfield. Sherman said he lost 12 officers and 65 men killed and 477 men wounded. The Confederates had left 68 wounded men, who were, along with the wounded Federals, carried to a nearby house that served as a field hospital.

General William J. Hardee
Source: Library of Congress

While Sherman was still in Averasboro, he received a letter from Grant saying that "Lee has depleted his army but very little recently, and I learn of none going south. Some regiments may have been detached, but I think no division or brigade. The determination seems to be to hold Richmond as long as possible."[83]

Grant said that he was sending him 5,000 more men, who were already on their way to join him. "My notion is, that you should get Raleigh as soon as possible, and hold the railroad from there back. From that point all North Carolina roads can be made useless to the enemy, without keeping up communications with the rear."[84]

From Averasboro, Sherman's left wing and Slocum turned east toward Goldsboro, the assembly point for Sherman's armies. With the 14th Corps leading, they were within 27 miles of Goldsboro and five miles from Bentonville when Sherman thought all danger was past and joined Howard and the right wing.[85]

A messenger arrived almost immediately saying that Slocum's army had run up against Johnston's whole army, which Johnston later said was 14,100 infantry and artillery. Not much against Sherman's 62,000 men, but Sherman's supplies were low, and he thought Johnston had many more troops than he did; so Sherman issued orders to avoid a general battle. Sherman sent orders for Slocum to fight

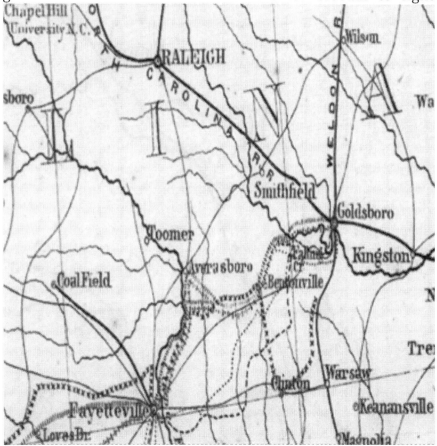

Sherman had arrived at his destination in Goldsboro, North Carolina. *Source: Library of Congress*

defensively from the west while the right wing approached Johnston's rear from the east.

The heaviest fighting at Bentonville was on March 19, but the skirmishing ended after three days, and Johnston's army retreated west. Sherman said in later years that if he had known how small Johnston's army was on March 21, he would have overwhelmed him instead of letting him go.[86]

Sherman, however, was eager to reach Goldsboro. "We have now been out six weeks, (since leaving Columbia) living precariously upon the collections of our foragers, our men dirty, ragged, and saucy, and we must rest and fix up a little," Sherman said.

The skirmishing since Sherman had entered North Carolina, including Averasboro and Bentonville, had been deadly, particularly for the Confederates. "Our entire losses thus far (killed, wounded, and prisoners) will be covered by 2,500, a great part of which are, as usual, slight wounds," Sherman said. "The enemy has lost more than double as many, and we have in prisoners alone fully two thousand."[87]

Sherman's troops rode toward Goldsboro, where his whole army was assembling on March 23 and March 24. Sherman notified Grant that rations and clothing were being replenished, and "I feel certain, from the character of the fighting, that we have got Johnston's army afraid of us. He himself acts with timidity and caution. His cavalry alone manifests spirit, but limits its operations to our stragglers and foraging parties. My marching columns of infantry do not pay the cavalry any attention, but walk right through it."[88]

Sherman said he could pretty clearly see how, "in one more move, we can checkmate Lee, forcing him to unite Johnston with him in the defense of Richmond, or to abandon the cause.[89]

4 GENERAL SHERMAN MEETS WITH LINCOLN

Leaving his army to rest and regroup in Goldsboro, North Carolina, General Sherman left on a train for Morehead City, where he boarded a small captured steamer on March 27 and steamed up to Fortress Monroe at Hampton, Virginia. Jefferson Davis would be a prisoner there within two months.

By mid-afternoon, Sherman was sitting with General Grant, his family and staff who were occupying a group of huts at City Point, Virginia, on the bank of the James River.

After visiting with Grant for several hours, Sherman learned that President Lincoln was on board the steamer River Queen lying at the wharf at City Point.

President Jefferson Davis would be in prison at Fortress Monroe, Virginia, by the end of May 1865. Source: Library of Congress

General Grant's headquarters were at City Point, Virginia, during the Seige of Petersburg, Source: Library of Congress

"We walked down to the wharf, went on board and found Mr. Lincoln alone, in the after-cabin," Sherman said. "He remembered me perfectly, and at once engaged in a most interesting conversation. He was full of curiosity about the many incidents of our great march, which had reached him officially and through the newspapers, and seemed to enjoy very much the more ludicrous parts— about the 'bummers,' and their devices to collect food and forage when the outside world supposed us to be starving; but at the same time he expressed a good deal of anxiety lest some accident might happen to the army in North Carolina during my absence."[90]

Sherman assured him that the army was in good camps in Goldsboro and that it would require several days of foraging to collect enough food for the march. "Having made a good, long, social visit, we took our leave and returned to General Grant's headquarters," Sherman said.[91]

When they returned to quarters at City Point, Grant's wife wanted to know if they had seen Mrs. Lincoln. "'No,' said the general. I did not ask for her;' and I added that I did not even know that she was on board. Mrs. Grant said, 'Well, you are a pretty pair!' and said their neglect was unpardonable. Grant said they would call again the next day and make amends for their unintended slight."[92]

The next day, after meeting with the principal officers of

President Abraham Lincoln
Source: Library of Congress

the Army and Navy, Sherman and Grant took a small tug from the wharf to visit the President again.

When Grant asked about Mrs. Lincoln, the President went to her stateroom, quickly returned and "begged us to excuse her as she was not well."[93]

Grant told the president that Sheridan was crossing the James River from the north by a pontoon bridge below City Point and that he was going to strike the Southside and Danville Railroads, the only remaining supply lines for Lee.

"I also explained the army at Goldsboro was strong enough to fight Lee's army and Johnston's combined, provided that General Grant could come up within a day or so; that if Lee would only remain in Richmond another fortnight, I could march up to Burkesville, when Lee would have to starve inside of his lines, or come out from his intrenchments (sic) and fight us on equal terms."[94]

Grant and Sherman agreed that one or the other would have to fight one more bloody battle—but it would be the last. "Mr. Lincoln exclaimed, more than once, that there had been blood enough shed, and asked if another battle could not be avoided," Sherman said. "I remember well to have said that we could not control that event; that this necessarily rested with our enemy; and I inferred that both Jeff. Davis and General Lee would be forced to fight one more desperate and bloody battle. I rather supposed it would fall on me, somewhere near Raleigh."[95]

Sherman asked the President what was to be done with the rebel armies when defeated. "And what should be done with the political leaders, such as Jeff. Davis, etc.," Sherman asked. "Should we allow them to escape, etc.? Lincoln said...all he wanted of us was to defeat the opposing armies, and to get the men composing the Confederate armies back to their homes, at work on their farms and in their shops."[96]

As for President Davis, Lincoln said he was hardly at liberty to speak his mind fully, but intimated that Davis ought to clear out, "escape the country," but it would not do for him to say so openly.[97]

Lincoln illustrated his meaning with a story. "A man once had taken the total-abstinence pledge. When visiting a friend, he was invited to take a drink, but declined, on the score of his pledge; when his friend suggested lemonade, which was accepted," Lincoln said. "In preparing the lemonade, the friend pointed to the brandy-bottle, and said the lemonade would be more palatable if he were to pour in a little brandy; when his guest said, if he could do so 'unbeknown' to him, he would 'not object.'" Sherman said he inferred from the illustration that Lincoln wanted Davis to escape "unbeknown" to him.[98]

Sherman said Lincoln assured him that in his mind he was all ready for the civil reorganization of affairs at the

N.C. Governor Zebulon Vance
Source: Library of Congress

South as soon as the war was over. "He distinctly authorized me to assure Governor (Zebulon) Vance and the people of North Carolina that, as soon as the rebel armies laid down their arms, and resumed their civil pursuits, they would at once be guaranteed all their rights as citizens of a common country; and that to avoid anarchy the State governments then in existence, with their civil functionaries, would be recognized by him as the government *de facto* till Congress could provide others."[99]

Lincoln made a similar illustration at an informal Cabinet meeting where the disposition of Davis and the other prominent Confederates was being discussed.

"Each member of the Cabinet gave his opinion," Lamon said. "Most of them were for hanging the traitors or for some severe punishment. Lincoln said nothing. Finally Joshua F. Speed, his old and confidential friend who had been invited to the meeting, said, 'I have heard the opinion of your Ministers and would like to hear yours.'"[100]

Lincoln launched into a story. "'Well, Josh,' replied Mr. Lincoln, 'when I was a boy in Indiana, I went to a neighbor's house one morning and found a boy of my own size holding a coon by a string. I asked him what he had and what he was doing. He says, 'It's a coon. Dad cotched six last night and killed all but this poor little cuss. Dad told me to hold him until he came back and I m afraid he's going to kill this one too, and, oh, Abe, I do wish he would get away.'

"Well, why don't you let him loose?" Lincoln asked.

"That wouldn't be right," the boy said, "and if I let him go, Dad would give me hell. But if he would get away himself, it would be all right."

Bridging from the "'coon" story, Lincoln said, "Now, if Jeff Davis and those other fellows will only get away, it will be all right. But if we should catch them and I should let them go, Dad would give me hell."[101]

After the meeting with Lincoln at City Point, Sherman was more than ever impressed by Lincoln's "kindly nature, his deep and earnest sympathy with the afflictions of the whole people, resulting from the war, and by the march of hostile armies through the South; and that his earnest desire seemed to be to end the war speedily, without more bloodshed or devastation, and to restore all the men of both sections to their homes."[102]

5 THE CONFEDERATE GOVERNMENT COLLAPSES

"Darkness seemed now to close swiftly over the Confederacy, and about a week before the evacuation of Richmond, Mr. Davis came to me and gently, but decidedly, announced the necessity for our departure," said President Davis' wife Varina Howell Davis.

"He said for the future his headquarters must be in the field, and that our presence would only embarrass and grieve, instead of comforting him."[103]

Davis urged her to leave at once and take their four children to a place of safety.[104] "If I live

Varina Howell Davis
Source: National Portrait Gallery, Washington, D.C.

you can come to me when the struggle is ended, but I do not expect to survive the destruction of constitutional liberty," he said. He had a little gold, and reserving a five-dollar piece for himself, he gave it all to her, as well as all the Confederate money due to him.[105]

Since she could carry only their clothing, Mrs. Davis sent all the household goods to a dealer for sale and received a large check, but she left in such haste the next day that the

The four children of Varina and Jefferson Davis left Richmond with Mrs. Davis. Source: Library of Congress

check was never cashed and she still had it in 1890 when she wrote her memoirs.[106] Davis's private secretary Burton N. Harrison was to accompany and "protect" Mrs. Davis with her four children, the oldest only 10 years old, and her sister on the trip to Charlotte, where they planned to stay an indefinite time. The daughters of Secretary of the Treasury George A. Trenholm were also in the entourage leaving Richmond.[107]

As Mrs. Davis packed to leave during the last week in March, she felt that "the deepest depression had settled upon the whole city; the streets were almost deserted."[108]

The day before her departure, Davis gave her a pistol and showed her how to load, aim, and fire it.[109]

"He was very apprehensive of our falling into the hands of the disorganized bands of troops roving about the country, and said, 'You can at least, if reduced to the last extremity, force your assailants to kill you, but I charge you solemnly to leave when you hear the enemy are approaching; and if you cannot remain undisturbed in our own country, make for the Florida coast and take a ship there for a foreign country.'"[110]

Midshipman James Morris was assigned to accompany the train as it left Richmond. He was a close friend of Mrs. Davis' youngest brother Midshipman Jefferson Davis Howell, and Morgan's brother had married Mrs. Davis' cousin.[111]

"There were no Pullman sleeping-coaches in those days," Morgan said, "and it was with great difficulty that an old creaky passenger car, long a stranger to paint and varnish, had been security for the wife of the chief magistrate of a nation of some fifteen or twenty millions of people. We at once entered the car and seated ourselves on the lumpy seats, which were covered with dingy and threadbare brownish red plush, very suggestive of the vermin with which it afterwards proved to be infested."[112]

President Davis soon entered the car and talked pleasantly and cheerfully with everyone before sitting and talking with his wife. After a two-hour wait, the train began "screeching and lurching" out of the station at 10 p.m. on Friday, March 31.[113]

James Morris
Source: Library of Congress

The train was barely out of sight of Richmond when the worn-out engine broke down, and Mrs. Davis and her family sat on the train through the night. After a 12-hour delay, they reached Danville[114] where they declined an invitation to stay over and instead remained on the train until they reached Charlotte.[115]

The train reached Charlotte on Tuesday, April 4, and Colonel Harrison hunted for shelter for Mrs. Davis and her family and friends.

As late as April 1, Jefferson Davis was concerned about getting iron manufactured at the Tredegar Iron Works in Richmond to provide shot and shell for the military. Source: Library of Congress

"The inhabitants, however, did not rush forward to offer this lady in distress hospitality as they might have done a year or two before misfortune had overtaken her," Morgan said.

"They seemed to take it for granted that the end of the Confederacy was at hand, although the news of the fall of Richmond (on April 2) did not reach them until two days after our arrival."[116]

However, a Mr. (Adam) Weil came forward and offered them a place (on the corner of North Brevard and East Fifth streets[117]) and brought them food while they were in Charlotte.[118]

Tredegar Iron Works were destroyed as the Federals entered Richmond on April 3, 1865. *Source: Library of Congress*

As hope died in the rank and file of the Confederate Army, Varina Davis said her husband's courage rose, and he continued trying to arrange supplies for the military but was "calm in the contemplation of the destruction of his dearest hopes, and the violent death he expected to be his."[119]

As late as April 1, Davis had written to Lee from Richmond, about the difficulty of finding enough iron to keep the Tredegar works in Richmond employed, and said: "There is also difficulty in getting iron even for shot and shell, but I hope this may for the present be overcome by taking some from the Navy, which under the altered circumstances may be spared. . . . The question is often asked, 'will we hold Richmond,' to which my only answer is, if we can; it is purely question of military power. The distrust is increasing, and embarrasses in many ways."[120]

But by then, the gloom in Richmond was impenetrable, Mrs. Davis said.[121]

6 GENERAL LEE SURRENDERS AT APPOMATTOX

The last spasm of Confederate resistance was an incessant two-week battle that started on March 25 with the charge of the troops of CSA General John Brown Gordon at Petersburg and ended with the last charge of General Lee's army on April 9 at Appomattox Courthouse.[122]

General John B. Gordon
Source: National Archives

"Night after night troops were marching, heavy guns were roaring, picket-lines were driven in and had to be reestablished," Gordon said, "and the great mortars from both Union and Con-federate works were hurling high in the air their ponderous shells, which crossed each other's paths and, with burning fuses, like tails of flying comets, descended in meteoric showers on the opposing intrenchments."[123]

On April 1, sleet and snow poured down on Lee's shelterless men in the trenches. Most of them were wearing mere rags, and some of them had burrowed into the earth for warmth. They had almost nothing to eat[124] because their allotment of one-quarter pound of rancid bacon and a little cornmeal had disappeared. Their rations had been reduced to one-sixth of the daily supply with very often no bacon at all because Sherman's troops had

General Ulysses S. Grant
Pastel portrait by John Miranda, Columbia, S.C.

destroyed their sup-ply lines—the railroad tracks in Georgia and the Carolinas.[125]

"In the last move-ment on the lines at Petersburg, Grant hurled his army of 124,000 brave and superbly equipped soldiers," Gordon said. "To resist them General Lee could then bring into line about 35,000 worn and wan but conse-crated fighters. Pos-sibly one half of these had been on the 1st and 2d of April, killed, wounded and captured, or the commands to which they belong had been so broken to pieces as to eliminate them from the effective forces. There was no hope for us except in retreat."[126]

From Lee as the commander-in-chief to the privates in the ranks, there was a deep and sincere religious feeling in Lee's army, Gordon said.

"Whenever it was convenient or practicable, these hungry but unyielding men were holding prayer meetings. Their supplications were fervent and often inspiring."[127]

Gordon said that even though the Confederates "fully comprehended the situation from an earthly or purely military point of view," they hoped to the last for some miraculous intervention.[128]

But no intervention occurred, and before daybreak on April 9, Lee, with General Fitz Lee's cavalry, moved forward to the attack.[129] "When confronted by Sheridan's cavalry, Lee drove them steadily before him and cap- tured two pieces of artillery," President Davis wrote later. "All seemed to be going well when (General Philip Henry) Sheridan with- drew from the field, and then, like the lifting of a curtain, Gordon beheld the Army of the James advancing

General Robert E. Lee
Pastel portrait by John Miranda, Columbia, S.C.

through the trees with ten times his number."[130] At the same time General James Longstreet, covering the rear and threatened by General George Meade with a superior force, found it impossible to reinforce Gordon, who, "stained with powder and exhausted by his recent battle, reared his knightly head and said, 'Tell General Lee my corps is

Wilmer McLean
Source: Library of Congress

47

Wilmer McLean's house at Appomattox. Source: Library of Congress

reduced to a frazzle.'"[131] Lee said, "There is nothing left but for me to go and see General Grant." And a flag of truce was raised to suspend hostilities pending the interview between the commanders.[132]

The generals met at the farmhouse of Wilmer McLean who had, during the battle of Manassas in July 1861, lived at McLean's Ford over Bull Run but had moved to Appomattox to escape the war.[133] "Fate directed the steps of both armies to his fancied secure and quiet retreat, and there the end was to come," Davis said.

"A suitable room having been prepared, and the two generals being seated, General Lee opened the interview by saying: 'General Grant, I deem it due to proper candor and frankness to say, at the very beginning of this interview, that I am not willing even to discuss any terms of surrender inconsistent with the honor of my

The Surrender at Appomattox in McLean's house: Shown (left to right) John Gibbon, George Armstrong Custer, Cyrus B. Comstock, Orville E. Babcock, Charles Marshall, Walter H. Taylor, Robert E. Lee, Philip Sheridan, Ulysses S. Grant, John Aaron Rawlins, Charles Griffin, unidentified, George Meade, Ely S. Parker, James W. Forsyth, Wesley Merritt, Theodore Shelton Bowers, Edward Ord. The man not identified in the picture's legend may be General Joshua Chamberlain, a hero at Gettysburg who presided over the formal surrender of arms by Lee's Army on April 12, 1865. Source: Library of Congress

army, which I am determined to maintain to the last.'"[134] Grant said, "I have no idea of proposing dishonorable terms. General; but I would be glad if you would   state what you consider honorable terms. Lee briefly stated the terms upon which he would be willing to surrender."[135]

Grant said he was satisfied with the terms, and the propositions were reduced to writing. Lee read the surrender document and several copies were made of the

SURRENDER OF GEN: LEE, AT APPOMATTOX C.H. V.ª APRIL 9ᵗ 1865.

Source: Library of Congress

paper by Lee's aide de camp Colonel Charles Marshall and Grant's secretary.[136] While this was being done, Generals

General Lee leaving McLean house after surrender. *Source: Library of Congress*

Grant and Lee exchanged a few words of civility, and the Federal generals who were present were introduced to Lee, but nothing bearing on the surrender was said.[137] After Grant signed his note, Lee conferred with Colonel Marshall, who wrote a brief note of acceptance of the proposed terms of surrender, which were as follows: "The officers to give their individual parole not to take arms against the Government of the United States until properly exchanged, and each company or regimental commander to sign a like parole for the men of their commands."[138] The arms, artillery, and public property were to be parked and stacked and turned over to the officers appointed to receive them. "This will not embrace the side-arms of the officers, nor their private horses or baggage.[139] This done, each officer and man would be allowed to return to their homes, not to be disturbed by the United States authority so long as they observe their parole, and the laws in force where they may reside."[140]

General Lee rose to leave, and, after bowing to the officers on the porch, beckoned to his orderly to lead up his horse. Descending the steps, he paused a moment and looked sadly out over the valley where his army lay, then mounted. General Grant, who had followed and descended a few steps, raised his hat in respectful salutation, as did those who stood upon the porch. Upon seeing this courtesy, General Lee, removing his hat, bowed low upon his horse's neck and rode away.[141]

"As soon as he was seen riding toward his army, whole lines of men rushed down to the roadside, and crowded around him to shake his hand," Davis would write later. "All tried to show him the veneration and esteem in which they held him. Filled with emotion he essayed to speak, but could only say, 'Men, we have fought through the war together. I have done the best I could for you. My heart is too full to say more.'"[142]

President Davis said that everyone knew the pathos of Lee's simple words, of that slight tremble in his voice, and that "it was no shame on anyone's manhood that something on a soldier's cheek washed off the stain of powder;" that "tears answered to those of our grand old chieftain," and that everyone could only grasp the hand of ' Uncle Robert' and pray 'God help you, General.'"[143]

At the time Lee surrendered, only 7,892 men of the army of Northern Virginia had arms in their hands. The total number, including those who reported afterward, was between 26,000 and 27,000. Grant's army was more than twice as large at 62,239.[144]

7 RICHMOND IS EVACUATED

General Lee's telegram announcing his speedy withdrawal from Petersburg and the consequent necessity for evacuating Richmond was handed to President Davis in St. Paul's Church on Sunday, April 2, and he left quietly.[145]

"The occurrence probably attracted attention, but the people had been beleaguered, had known me too often to receive notice of threatened attacks, and the Congregation of St. Paul's was too refined to make a scene

President Jefferson Davis was attending St. Paul's Church in Richmond, Virginia, on April 2, 1865. Source: Library of Congress

The Treasury Building in Richmond *Source: Library of Congress*

at anticipated danger," Davis said.[146]

He went to his offices on the top floor of the Treasury Building at the foot of Capitol Square and assembled the heads of departments and bureaus as far as they could be found on a day when all the offices were closed. He gave instructions for the evacuation of Richmond that night to be simultaneous with Lee's retreat from Petersburg.[147]

"The event was foreseen, and some preparations had been made for it, though, as it came sooner than was expected, there was yet much to be done," Davis said. Most of the records and documents were on the second floor, where the offices of the state department and cabinet room were located. "The executive papers were arranged for removal," he said, and he and his staff worked late in the afternoon.[148]

Down on the first floor where the treasury department and printing presses for Confederate money were located, treasury officials scrambled to pack the contents of the Confederate treasury, which was estimated at $500,000 in gold and silver.

The chests also included Confederate paper money that was later estimated to be in the millions by the last acting Secretary of the Treasury Micajah H. Clark.[149]

Micajah Henry Clark, the last acting Secretary of the Treasury.
Source: Louisiana Research Collection, Tulane University

Chests containing some of the Confederate treasury had been moved from Richmond to Columbia and Newberry, South Carolina, at the end of 1864, according to Colonel D. A. Dickert of Newberry.[150]

"Just before Sherman began his march through the Carolinas, the 'treasury' makers split up, one part coming to Newberry," he said.[151]

James Jones was Davis' bodyguard and paid servant who would continue to stay with Davis during the two years he was imprisoned at Fortress Monroe. When Jones was 80 years old in 1913, he said that some of the treasure was moved out of Richmond in the days before the government fell.

"When defeat became certain, just before the close of the war, during which I had constantly served as Col. Davis's body guard and servant, he intrusted to me the sum of thirteen million dollars in gold, silver coin and English notes, to convey from Richmond to South Carolina," Jones said. "This sum was under my exclusive charge for four weeks."[152]

Jones said that no one knew about his mission "except Col. Davis, Capt. Parker of South Carolina, who was a Confederate officer to whom I was to deliver it, and myself. I had it in two trunks, and conveyed it on the railroad as common baggage although I guarded it to its destination in Newberry, South Carolina, where I delivered it to Captain Parker," he said.[153]

A month later, Parker, who was from New York, not South Carolina, did go to Newberry, as Jones said, but Parker never acknowledged receiving any additional treasure when he arrived there. However, $13 million was the exact amount mentioned by Sherman as the sum of money that General Henry Halleck and other Federal officials believed was available to Sherman to let Davis escape through North Carolina.[154]

Sherman scoffed at the implication that he and his armies could be bribed but never denied the allegations, and the fate of the two chests of treasure that Jones said he delivered to Newberry is unknown. Parker, who would guard the $950,000 bank and treasury gold and specie (coins) that left Richmond on April 2 until he turned it over to Postmaster and Secretary of the Treasury John Reagan in Washington, Georgia, would in later years question the distribution and accounting of Confederate treasure. "In my opinion a good deal of the money was never accounted for, and there remains what sailors call 'Flemish account' of it," (an old British slang for a sum of money less than expected).[155]

Additionally, at least three stories emerged about the solid silver Confederate seals and engraving plates that were smuggled out of Richmond. Secretary of State Judah Benjamin entrusted most of his records to his clerk William J. Bromwell, including a silver seal, which Mrs. Bromwell hid in her skirts.[156]

The silver seal that had been hidden by Mrs. Bromwell passed through several hands before being sold in 1912 to the Confederate Museum at Richmond for $3,000, which is where it is today in its leather case.[157]

Secretary of State Judah Benjamin
Source: Library of Congress

Benjamin threw the provisional Confederate seal plates into the Savannah River[158] in a spot called the Hominy Pot, an eddy at a sharp bend on the South Carolina side of the Savannah River.[159] And the embossing

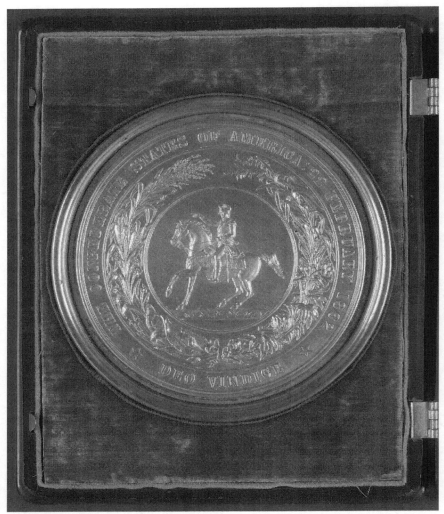

The official silver Confederate seal *Source: Library of Congress*

press is reported to be in the National Trust Museum in St. George's Bermuda.[160] However, Davis' servant Jim Jones would claim in 1913 that he had hidden at Davis' direction a different 10-pound silver seal that apparently has never been found. After returning to Richmond from the Newberry trip, "Col. Davis intrusted me with the mission of hiding the great seal, beyond the possibility of resurrection," Jones said. In describing the manner and the emotions of Mr. Davis while entrusting him with this charge, ("the tears coming into his eyes") when he spoke, Jones said, "James, I hereby hand you solemnly and sacredly, the seal of the Confederate States of America.

The Southern government is about to fall. This seal, which we must and do hold sacred and undefilable, must be secreted, where no man in future shall profane it, by public gaze and examination, I intrust this mission to you. I hereby charge you with this seal's disappearance. Hide it and let no man know where it is. Tell not even me. And let the secret die with you."161

Secretary of the Navy Stephen Mallory *Source: Library of Congress*

The secret of that seal appears to have died with Jones because apparently no one has found the seal that he described as being "a large silver slab that weighed about 10 pounds" that was made in London and was brought to this country by blockade-runners.162

While packing to leave Richmond with the remnants of the Confederacy, Davis' faithful friend Micajah H. Clark said, "I saw an organized government disintegrate and fall to pieces little by little, until there was only left a single member of the cabinet, (Davis') private secretary, a few members of his staff, a few guides and servants, to

CSS Patrick Henry was set on fire by Confederates as they were leaving Richmond. Source: Library of Congress

represent what had been a powerful government, "which had sustained itself against the soldiery of all nations of the earth."[163] At the end, Clark would, as the last acting Secretary of the Treasury, dispense large sums of gold and silver to the military and other government officials and burn what he described as "millions of dollars worth of Confederate money" on the flight through Georgia.[164]

While Davis and his aides were packing on April 2, Confederate Navy Captain William H. Parker received orders soon after 2 p.m. from Secretary of the Navy Stephen K. Mallory to blow up the *Patrick Henry*, which was docked in the James River. The steamer was the midshipmen's school ship and the seat of the academy.[165]

"We had on board some sixty midshipmen and a full corps of professors," Parker said. "The midshipmen were well drilled in infantry tactics, and all of the professors save one had served in the army or navy."[166]

Parker had been the superintendent of the Confederate States Naval Academy from 1863-1865.[167] After ordering the ship to be burned, Parker went to the Navy Department where Mallory told him the city was being evacuated and that the corps would be in charge of guarding the Confederate treasure.

"The city was to be evacuated that evening and my command was to take charge of the Confederate treasure and convey it to Danville," Parker said. "Everything was being packed up for carrying off about the departments though a good many things had been sent away in March in anticipation of this event. In the city those who had anything to do were at work at it."[168]

Although the gold and specie from the treasury and banks that Parker escorted out of Richmond would become the stuff of legends, it was only a small part of the government and civilian financial holdings held in the Confederacy and foreign countries. Most of it would fall into the hands of looting Federal armies and the U.S. government, which would soon send agents and soldiers

The Charlotte Federal mint became the Mint Museum of Art.
Image in the public domain.

accompanied by a wide-range of imposters into the former Confederacy to tax and seize gold, cotton and other commodities while an avalanche of lawsuits was launched against banks, civilians and England.[169]

The Confederate government had mints in Dahlonega, Georgia, and New Orleans, Louisiana. The federal Branch Mint at Dahlonega had $23,716 in gold and silver when it was taken over by the Confederate States of America in 1861. During the autumn of 1862, the mint turned $40,000 in gold and silver from New Orleans, Louisiana, into bars for shipment to Augusta, Georgia. At the same time, Confederate officials seized from the Bank of Louisiana in Columbus $2.3 million in gold and $216,000 in silver specie that had traveled there after New Orleans fell to Union forces.[170]

Gold from civilians made Macon, Georgia, second only to Richmond as a Confederate depository. By the end of the war, Union General E. L. Molineux in Macon had taken charge of $275,000 in confiscated gold and silver, including some that Union soldiers plundered from civilians. This total included at least $35,000 worth of coins and bullion that had been left for hungry Confederates returning home. Molineux also seized $188,000 from the assets of the Central Railroad Bank of Savannah. He did not find $200,000 in gold coins from the Georgia State Bank of Savannah that were hidden in Macon, but the federal government confiscated more than $500,000 in assets from the Bank of Tennessee and its branches in Augusta at the end of the war.[171]

The Charlotte Mint had been seized by the Charlotte Grays on April 20, 1861, after the firing on Fort Sumter and converted to Confederate headquarters.[172] It no longer stored gold, but local banks contained more than $250,000 in gold that was hidden in the woods as the

Evans and Cogswell Confederate Printing Plant in Columbia, S.C., was pillaged and burned by Sherman's troops. Courtesy of South Caroliniana Library, University of South Carolina, Columbia

Federals approached.[173] The contents of hundreds of Confederate banks containing thousands of dollars in gold and money and other valuables disappeared during and after the war by looting and pillaging and at the end of the war by seizure from Federal treasury agents.

The bank vaults in Columbia, South Carolina, were "crammed with securities, gold, silver and jewelry" because everyone thought Columbia was one of the safest places in the Confederacy,[174] but they were looted while the city was being burned by Sherman's troops on the night of February 17, 1865.

The Confederate Printing Plant in Columbia, South Carolina, containing thousands of dollars in Confederate money, was plundered by Sherman's troops during the burning of Columbia. The General remembered that his men gambled wildly with the specie found in the Confederate Printing Plant in Columbia before it was burned. He wrote about it in later years, but he never said anything about the distribution of the gold and silver pillaged from civilians and burned-out banks in his campaign through Georgia and the Carolinas. "The dies (of the printing plant) had been carried away, but about sixty hand presses remained," Sherman said. "There was also found an immense quantity of money, in various states of manufacture, which our men spent and gambled with in the most lavish manner."[175]

The method of distribution of the looted gold, silver and other valuables was apparently never documented in any official reports, but while Lieutenant Thomas G. Myers was camped in Winnsboro, South Carolina, after the burning of Columbia, he wrote a letter on February 26, 1865, that gave exact details and named names.

Addressed to his wife in Boston, the letter described the regulations of robbing and stealing valuables and the way the plunder was divided in Sherman's army. The details of the letter are supported by stories from dozens of citizens in Columbia who had been violently robbed of all gold, valuables and jewelry, and Myers implicated Sherman and described his role in the division of loot.

Myers wrote:

"...We have had a glorious time in this State. Universal license to burn and plunder was the order of the day. The chivalry have been stript of most of their valuables. Gold watches, silver pitchers, cups, spoons, forks, etc., etc., are as common in camp as blackberries. The terms of plunder are as follows:

The valuables procured we estimate by companies. Each company is required to exhibit the result of its operations at any given place. One-fifth and first choice falls to the share of the Commander-in-chief and staff, one-fifth to field officers of regiments, and three-fifths to the company. Officers are not allowed to join these expeditions without disguising themselves as privates. ... Officers over the rank of Captain are not made to put their plunder in the estimate for general distribution.

"This is very unfair, and for that reason, in order to protect themselves, subordinate officers and privates keep back everything that they can carry about their person, such as rings, ear-rings, breast-pins, etc., of which, if ever I live to get home, I have about a quart—I am not joking—I have at least a quart of jewelry for you and all the girls, and some No. 1 diamond rings and pins among them."[176]

The jewelry, gold and silver stolen by Federal troops would never be reported and are a vast part of the Confederate gold lost during the Civil War.

Myers described the enormous amount of treasure hauled out of Columbia. "...We took gold and silver enough from the d___d rebels to have redeemed their infernal currency twice over," he wrote.

"This, (the currency) whenever we come across it we burn as we consider it utterly worthless," Myers said. "I wish all the jewelry this army has could be carried to the old Bay State. It would deck her out in glorious style, but alas! it will be scattered all over the North and Middle States."

Myers was particular to point out that Sherman was participating in the division of treasure that was stolen during his campaign. "Gen. Sherman has silver and gold enough to start a bank," he wrote. "His share in gold watches and chains alone at Columbia was two hundred and seventy-five ($275), (which in today's dollars would be worth about $4,125),[177].... He cautioned his wife not to show the letter out of the family.

As a mark of authenticity, Myers even named three of their victims. He described stealing the gold watch and other valuables of William F. DeSaussure, who later became mayor of Columbia, and the "Misses Jamison" who were the daughters of General David Flavel Jamison of Orangeburg, president of the Secession Convention. The daughters had apparently fled to Georgia where their jewelry was stolen, and their home was burned later as Sherman's troops passed through Orangeburg.[178]

William F. DeSaussure's gold watch was stolen by Sherman's troops and he was made to "fork over liberally." He later became mayor of Columbia, S.C.
Source: City of Columbia

However, the most famous Civil War treasure—the gold and silver that people still hope to find in some secreted spot—was loaded onto trains in Richmond on the night that President Davis and his Confederate government began their retreat to the Confederate Trans-Mississippi Department on the west side of the Mississippi River.[179]

Parker arrived at the depot at 6 p.m. with his officers and men—"perhaps something over one hundred, all told," he said,—and was put in charge of a train of cars on which was being packed Confederate treasure and the money belonging to the banks of Richmond.

The treasure train filled quickly with the official records of the Confederacy as well as "—some say hundreds—of crates and barrels containing gold and silver coins, bullion, and a substantial amount of fine jewelry donated to the Cause by women across the South," Morgan said. Although all the hard currency reserves of the Confederacy that had been stored in Richmond were on board, Secretary of the Treasury George A. Trenholm was not with the treasure, Parker said.

"The senior officer of the Treasury present was a cashier, and he informed me, to the best of my recollection, that there was about $500,000 in gold, silver, and bullion."[180]

Secretary of War John Breckinridge
Source: Library of Congress

In addition there was more than $450,000 in gold from Richmond bank reserves, taken to keep it from falling into the hands of the invading Yankees, according to Parker.[181]

Even though Parker believed that he was guarding almost $1 million in hard currency of gold, silver and bullion, he never saw the contents of the boxes. "I saw the boxes containing it many times in the 'weary thirty days' I had it under my protection,'" he said, but he never actually "saw the coin."[182]

However, on April 27, U.S. General Henry Halleck said that bankers in Richmond had told the Federals that "specie taken with them is estimated here at from six to thirteen million dollars."[183]

In addition to not seeing the contents, Parker never mentioned that the treasure train also contained enormous quantities of Confederate money even though he would later describe the large amounts that he threw away on their route back from Augusta, Georgia. And

Captain M.H. Clark of Clarksville, Tennessee, who was acting secretary of the treasury at the time of the surrender, described burning huge amounts of Confederate money from the treasure train in Washington, Georgia. "I also directed him to burn the Confederate notes in the presence of General (John) Breckinridge and myself," Clark said.[184]

Clark said when he reached Washington, Georgia on May 4, "I obtained permission from General Breckinridge and Mr. (John) Reagan to burn a mass of currency and bonds, and burnt millions in their presence. Before reaching town I was halted by Major R. J. Moses, to turn over to him the specie which President Davis, before he left, had ordered to be placed at the disposal of the Commissary Department, to feed the paroled soldiers and stragglers passing through, to prevent their burdening a section already stripped of supplies. I turned over to Major Moses the wagons and silver bullion, and all of the escort except about ten men," Clark said.[185]

Elaborate descriptions and detailed accountings have focused on the fate and distribution of the $950,000 in gold and silver on Parker's train that had been in the Confederate treasury and banks in Richmond. But no one counted the by-then worthless "millions" of dollars in Confederate money that was burned or thrown away along the route by Parker and Clark. Nor was there any accounting for the gold and other valuables stolen and destroyed by Federal troops in their paths through the Confederacy, including Columbia, South Carolina, and other cities whose banks were looted and burned.

8 THE TREASURE TRAIN LEAVES RICHMOND

The President's train was to precede the treasure train, which was expected to be the last out of the city on April 2, Captain Parker said. "Both trains were packed, not only inside but on top, on the platforms, on the engine, everywhere in fact where standing room could be found, and those who could not get that hung on by their eyelids. I placed sentinels at the doors of the depot finally and would not let another soul enter."[186]

Finally loaded, the special train carrying the President and members of the Confederate Cabinet creaked out of Richmond late on the night of April 2 for Danville, Virginia. "Although the news was bleak, it was the hope of all on board that the struggle could be continued," said Captain Parker.[187]

Shortly after midnight the second train left the Richmond station to follow the fleeing government toward Danville. Secretary of War John Breckenridge stayed at the depot with Parker until the treasure train left the station before riding out of the city on horseback.

The treasure train was heavily loaded and crowded with passengers—even on top of the cars and on the steps—and was moving very slowly. "How the train got by Amelia Courthouse without falling in with (General Philip) Sheridan's men was a mystery," Parker said.[188]

The trains carrying Davis and the remnants of the Confederate government were headed for Danville because he was expecting General Lee to meet him there with his army.[189] Davis and the first train arrived in Danville the next morning on Monday, April 3, followed by the treasure train that afternoon. Davis was a guest in the home of Major W.T. Sutherlin where Davis established the last capitol of the Confederacy and held a full cabinet

President Davis stayed at the home of Major W.T. Sutherlin in Danville, the last capitol of the Confederacy. Photo by Pat McNeely

meeting. Only Breckinridge was absent. Admiral Raphael Semmes arrived that night with the officers of the James River squadron and Parker on the last train out of Richmond.[190]

When Lee had not arrived by April 5, Davis wrote to his wife that he had tried in vain to communicate with General Lee and had postponed writing "in the hope that I would soon be able to speak to you with some confidence of the future."[191] The Mayor and Council had offered him assistance with lodging and had "very handsomely declared their unabated confidence. I do not wish to leave Virginia, but cannot decide on my movements until those of the army are better developed," he said.[192]

Although neither Davis nor Lee knew it at the time, Lee would soon be forced to surrender because of a significant blunder made by the Confederates while they were evacuating Richmond. Soon after his entrance into the city, Federal General Godfrey Weitzel had found a letter from General Lee giving the condition of the Army of Northern Virginia and what he proposed to do should it become necessary to withdraw from the lines before Richmond and Petersburg. The letter was sent immediately to General Grant.[193]

In answer to some doubts about the authenticity of the letter, General Henry Washington Benham replied, "Oh, there is no doubt about the letter, for I saw it myself."[194]

Davis had the impression at the time or afterward, that this letter was a confidential communication to the Secretary of War in answer to a resolution of the Confederate Congress asking for information in 1865. "When I mentioned this statement of General Benham to General Lee, sometime afterward, the latter said, 'This accounts for the energy of the enemy's pursuit. The first day after we left the lines he seemed to be entirely at sea with regard to our movements. After that, though I never worked so hard in my life to withdraw our armies in safety, (Grant) displayed more energy, skill, and judgment in his movements than I ever knew him to display before.'"[195]

With a blueprint of Lee's planned movements in hand, Grant's armies were able to outmaneuver Lee at every turn. Encumbered by a large wagon train, Lee's march was slow and his trains were attacked again and again by federal cavalry.[196]

By April 4, Lee's army had reached Amelia Court House without rations, and on April 5, Lee tried to continue his retreat toward Danville, hoping to form a junction with Johnston's army. The Federals headed him off, and the march turned toward Lynchburg where Lee had expressed his belief that he could carry on the war for twenty years.[197]

Meanwhile the midshipmen bivouacked near the railroad station in Danville. "We were very anxious to hear from General Lee's army as may well be imagined and for some days had fears for General Breckenridge's safety," but Breckenridge had finally arrived on horseback with his staff on Wednesday, April 5.[198] On April 6, the Confederate rear guard was attacked by a large force of Federals, and Generals G.W.C. Lee, Richard Ewell, James Patton Anderson and others were captured.[199]

Also, on Thursday, April 6, while Davis was still waiting anxiously in Danville to hear from Lee, Secretary of the Navy Stephen Mallory ordered Parker to move the treasure to Charlotte, North Carolina. He was to deposit it in the Mint and await further orders.[200] The Mint had been established on West Trade Street in 1835 during the height of a gold rush in the Charlotte area.[201]

Before leaving Danville, Parker asked Mallory about seeing Secretary of the Treasury Trenholm in reference to the Confederate treasurer and assistant treasurer accompanying the treasure as its appointed custodians.[202]

"It was their duty to be with it at this time. I did not think it right that it should be left with a Teller as the senior civil officer," Parker said. "This was a source of annoyance to me from that time forward. Not that I had anything against the Teller. I did not know him but I thought it was a time when every man should be made to do his duty. It was not a time to be falling sick by the wayside as some high officials were beginning to do."[203]

Parker's veiled reference was to Trenholm, who had fallen ill in Richmond before the train left the station.

Parker reported that some of the treasure was taken

at Danville *"by authority,"* but he never said how much.[204] "We did not unpack the treasure from the cars at Danville except that taken for the use of the Government at the time," he said. "How much was taken or for whom it was taken I never knew. It was not my business to inquire."[205]

When Acting Secretary of the Treasury Clark rode out to General Basil Duke's camp near Sandersonville, Georgia, on May 4, the remaining specie taken out of the treasury in Richmond was turned over to him. Although Parker said the Confederate treasury contained $500,000 when it left Richmond, Clark would report later that the treasury contained only $327,022.90 when it left Danville. Out of that, $39,000 was paid to soldiers in Greensboro, so that the treasury contained $288,022.90 when he took over outside of Washington, Georgia. By his accounting, $172,977.10 did not leave Danville.

Clark made no mention of 39 kegs of Mexican silver dollars left in Danville that the Confederacy is believed to have received through the sale of cotton to Mexico. The Mexican coins had been transported to Danville, and when the Davis party was forced to continue on to Greensboro, the more than 9,000 pounds of silver would have slowed down the procession. The treasure train, which was guarded by Parker, was already loaded to capacity and left for Charlotte ahead of Davis and his entourage, and some believe even today that the kegs of silver dollars were buried in Danville, in one of the city-owned cemeteries like Green Hill, which was established in 1863 and is near a railroad track.[206]

Efforts are still being made today to gain permission to dig in the cemetery, but their requests are being denied by the city of Danville.[207] The presence of Mexican silver in Danville would have been possible and logical because of the extensive cotton trading with Mexico that was being

The city-owned Green Hill Cemetery in Danville was established in 1863. Photo by Pat McNeely

operated by General Kirby Smith, who had established an economic empire in the Trans-Mississippi Department where Davis was headed.[208]

In any case, caches of the silver coins have reportedly been detected at several locations in the Danville search area, according to History News Network. A Colorado company, hired by a private individual, performed a geophysical survey and employed pulse induction instruments to identify the locations of the silver and a small amount of gold. If the silver coins are still in Danville cemeteries, they may never be found because they are buried on city-owned land, and Danville officials, concerned about disturbing graves, continue to refuse all requests to dig, even test holes, the network said. The value of the silver today is estimated at $16 million, according to History News Network.[209]

Not realizing that he was leaving a controversy behind that would rage for more than 150 years, Parker left Danville with the treasure train around April 6 on his way to Greensboro where he would remain for a day before continuing on to Charlotte.[210]

9 GENERAL SHERMAN ENDS HIS CAMPAIGN

Goldsboro, North Carolina, was the end of the campaign that General Sherman had designed in Atlanta, and he was anticipating joining General Grant's field of operation. As Richmond was falling on April 2, the Confederate leaders began making their way through Virginia and North Carolina toward Georgia.

General William T. Sherman
Source: Library of Congress

By April 5, Sherman was in Goldsboro, relaxing and saying, "My army is now here, pretty well clad and provided, divided into three parts, of two corps each— much as our old Atlanta army was." He was making plans to move on in a few days and to open communications with Grant, but he was waiting for more supplies and the arrival of men who were marching up from the coast.[211]

Sherman was reviewing with satisfaction his campaign through Georgia and the Carolinas. "Thus was concluded one of the longest and most important marches ever made by an organized army in a civilized country," Sherman wrote. "The distance from Savannah to Goldsboro is four hundred and twenty five miles, and the route traversed five large navigable rivers, viz., the Edisto, Broad, Catawba, Pedee, (sic) and Cape Fear, at either of which a comparatively small force, well-handled, should have made the passage most difficult, if not impossible," he said. [212]

"The country generally was in a state of nature, with innumerable swamps, with simply mud roads, nearly every mile of which had to be corduroyed. In our route, we had captured Columbia, Cheraw, and Fayetteville, important cities and depots of supplies, had compelled the evacuation of Charleston City and harbor, had utterly broken up all the railroads of South Carolina, and had consumed a vast amount of food and forage, essential to the enemy for the support of his own armies. [213]

"We had in mid-winter accomplished the whole journey of four hundred and twenty five miles in fifty days, averaging 10 miles per day, allowed ten lay-days, and had reached Goldsboro with the army in superb order, and the (supply) trains almost as fresh as when we had started from Atlanta."[214]

After his visit with Grant and the President at City Point, Sherman headed back to Raleigh to resume the march toward Grant's field of operations. He knew there was no force that could delay his progress, unless Lee could elude Grant at Petersburg and make junction with Johnston, and thus united meet Sherman alone. "I had no fear even of that event," he said.[215]

As Sherman headed for Raleigh, North Carolina, a train arrived with a letter from Governor Zebulon Vance asking for protection for the citizens of Raleigh.[216] Sherman was planning to move on Ashboro and Greensboro to cut off Confederate retreat lines through Salisbury and Charlotte, but he issued orders to stop destroying railroads, mills, cotton and produce. He said troops would be permitted to continue foraging, "only more care should be taken not to strip the poorer classes too closely."[217]

10 THE TREASURE TRAIN REACHES S.C.

As Captain Parker approached Salisbury, North Carolina, he saw cavalry descending the hills in the vicinity and stopped to reconnoiter. but they turned out to be Confederates and passed on. "We reached Charlotte about the 8th and I deposited the money in the mint as directed and left it in the custody of its proper officers," Parker said. "I thought I was rid of it forever."[218]

While Parker was depositing gold in Charlotte, General George Stoneman's Union cavalry, farther west in North Carolina, fought skirmishes at Shallow Ford and near Mocksville on April 11.[219] And on April 12, Stoneman's federal cavalry moved toward Salisbury, just 45 miles from Charlotte, and charged some 3,000 Confederates at Grant's Creek. About 1,300 Confederates were captured and Stoneman's cavalry occupied Salisbury.[220]

General George Stoneman
Source: Library of Congress

Stoneman's cavalry had left Greenville in East Tennessee at the end of March to begin the expedition that would end in Salisbury. Their orders were to destroy the railroads and Lee's supply lines from North Carolina

General George Stoneman became well known in 1863 when he was assigned to raid deeply into General Robert E. Lee's territory to destroy vital railroad lines. Source: Library of Congress

into Virginia.[221] Parker remained in Charlotte several days before going to the telegraph office to send a message to the Secretary of the Navy.

"I found the wires had been cut by General Stoneman who was then in possession of Salisbury with his command," Parker said. "It was supposed he would obtain information there concerning the treasure and that he would soon make his appearance in Charlotte where there were no troops to oppose him. I was the senior naval officer present on duty in Charlotte and had to decide as to the necessary steps to preserve the treasure."[222]

General P.G.T. Beauregard
Source: *Library of Congress*

President Davis was still in Greensboro, just 50 miles north of Salisbury, which was in a direct line on the route from Greensboro to Charlotte, where Davis was headed. Parker, believing that Stoneman's men were between him and the President and might be pushing toward Charlotte, decided to take the money out of the Mint and transport it further south, probably to Macon, Georgia, he was thinking.[223]

"Mrs. President Davis and family were in town and I called to offer her the protection of my command," Parker said. "After some demur she decided to accompany us. I rather pressed the point as I feared she would be captured and I could not bear the idea of that. We found in the naval storehouse here large quantities of sugar, coffee, bacon, and flour and I took enough to support my command several months. It was a most fortunate proceeding on my part" as the results showed later.[224]

The storekeeper objected to his requests and wanted requisitions approved by the Secretary of the Navy. "But I told him it was no time for red tape and that moreover I had the force and intended to have it," Parker said. "He gracefully acquiesced and rendered us all the assistance in his power in selecting the best of the stores."[225]

A company of uniformed men primarily from the navy yard volunteered to accompany Parker. "These men were principally from Portsmouth, Va and they remained with me to the end," Parker said.[226] Before leaving Danville for Greensboro, the President telegraphed to General Johnston that Lee had surrendered on April 9.

Having laid in supplies from the naval store house, Parker and the Davis family and friends left Charlotte on the treasure train, which arrived on April 12 in Chester, South Carolina.[227]

While Stoneman was occupying Salisbury, the President and his party were arriving in Greensboro, where Davis asked Johnston to meet him for a conference in the home that was General Beauregard's headquarters. "In compliance with my request, General Johnston came to Greensborough, N.C., and with General Beauregard met me and most of my Cabinet there," Davis said.[228] Davis held two meetings with his cabinet April 12-13 at the home of J. T. Wood at South Elm Street at McGee Street in Greensboro.[229]

In spite of the daily bad news, Davis continued to be optimistic about the future of the Confederacy.

"Though sensible of the effect of the surrender of the Army of Northern Virginia, and the consequent discouragement which these two events would produce, I did not despair," Davis said. "We had effective armies in the field, and a rich and productive territory both east and west of the Mississippi, whose citizens had shown no desire to surrender. Ample supplies had been collected in the railroad depots, and much still remained to be placed at our disposal when needed."[230]

At the first conference in Greensboro of the members of the Cabinet and the generals, Johnston said he wanted to open a correspondence with Sherman with a view toward suspending hostilities, and thereby permit the civil authorities to enter into arrangements to end the war.[231]

Davis resisted the plan. "As long as we were able to keep the field, I had never contemplated a surrender, except upon the terms of a belligerent, and never expected a Confederate army to surrender while it was able either to fight or to retreat," he said. "Lee had surrendered only when it was impossible for him to do either, and had proudly rejected Grant's demand until he found himself surrounded and his line of retreat cut off."[232]

The reluctant Davis was not optimistic about negotiations between the federal civil authorities and those of the Confederacy, believing that, even if Sherman should agree to such a proposition, his Government would not ratify it, (which is exactly what happened).[233]

"After having distinctly announced my opinions, I yielded to the judgment of my constitutional advisers, and consented to permit Johnston to hold a conference with Sherman," he said.[234]

"Johnston left for his army headquarters, and I, expecting that he would soon take up his line of retreat, which his superiority in cavalry would protect from harassing pursuit, proceeded with my Cabinet and staff to Charlotte, N.C."[235]

On the way, a dispatch was received from Johnston stating that Sherman had agreed to a conference and asking that Secretary of War General Breckinridge should return for the meeting.[236]

By then, the railroad tracks south of Greensboro had been destroyed by General Stoneman's troops as they swept in from western North Carolina. No longer able to ride by train, President Davis and

General Joseph Johnston
Source: Library of Congress

his escort left Greensboro on horses and wagons on April 15, heading south to Salisbury and Charlotte on their way to the Trans-Mississippi Department west of the Mississippi River.[237]

11 MRS. DAVIS AND THE TREASURE REACH S.C.

While General Johnston was meeting with General Sherman in Durham, North Carolina, the leaders of the Confederate government, with Federal troops nearby, were passing through North Carolina. Captain Parker and Mrs. Davis crossed into South Carolina first, having ridden the train into Chester, South Carolina, where the railroad lines south into South Carolina ended. All rails in the path of Sherman's troops on his campaign through Georgia and South Carolina had been destroyed.

"As time wore on all the news we received was of that kind which is reputed to travel fast, but did not over the broken railways and tangled and trailing telegraph wires," Mrs. Davis said.[238]

Although Lee had surrendered on April 9, Mrs. Davis still had not heard the news. "At last came the dreadful rumor that Lee was retreating, and the President and his cabinet were on their way to Charlotte to meet General Johnston and his army," she said.[239]

"I felt then that I must obey Mr. Davis's solemn charge, and also that I might embarrass him sadly by remaining there. That night the treasure train of the Confederacy and that of the Richmond banks, escorted by the midshipmen under the accomplished and gallant Captain Parker, came through Charlotte; and as among the escort were my brother Jefferson and Mr. Davis's grandnephew, and there seemed to be a panic imminent, I decided to go with my children and servants on the extra train provided for the treasure, which could only run as far as Chester, as the road was broken."[240]

The little command had only a short breathing spell at Charlotte "as the enemy were fast approaching and there was little time for them left in which to make a 'get away,'" Morgan said.[241]

General John Bell Hood (left) and General James Chesnut
Source: Library of Congress

They left Charlotte in the cars on April 12 and arrived at Chester, South Carolina, the next morning where they were met by Generals John S. Preston, John Bell Hood and James Chesnut.[242]

Preston said, "We of this day have no future, but we can worthily bear defeat; anything that man can do I will for you or the President."[243]

Hood said: "If I have lost my leg and also lost my freedom, I am miserable indeed."[244]

And Chesnut bowed his head and said: "Let me help you if I can, it is probably the last service I can render."[245]

"And these three types of Southern gentlemen formed a noble picture as they stood calm in the expectation of our great woe," Parker said.[246]

Parker persuaded Mrs. Davis to leave Chester under the protection of the midshipmen. Since the rails south of Chester had been destroyed by Sherman's men,[247] Parker

Woodward Baptist Church, located 5 miles south of Chester, S.C.
Photo by Pat McNeely

commandeered some wagons that he loaded with Mrs. Davis and her family and friends. After packing the gold and papers, he formed a wagon train to begin the trek across country toward Newberry, South Carolina.[248]

Erroneously supposing that Stoneman would follow, Parker was eager to get out of town and prepared to repel an attack by day and night. He published orders regulating their march, declared martial law and made every man carry a musket. "I had about 150 fighting men under my command and expected if attacked that we could give a good account of ourselves," Parker said.[249] The Treasury clerks, bank officers, and others made up a third company.[250]

"What a distressing spectacle this train of three or four wagons, hauled by broken-down and leg-weary mules, must have presented," Morgan said. "A platoon of the middies marched in front of the singular procession, acting as an advance guard. Another detachment followed the wagons, serving as a rear guard, and on either side of the train marched the rest of the youngsters. And not far away, on either flank and in their rear, hovered deserters waiting either for an opportunity or the necessary courage to pounce upon the, to them, untold wealth which those wagons contained."[251]

As the train of wagons rolled south out of Chester toward Fairfield County, the ambulance was too heavily laden in the deep mud, and as Mrs. Davis' maid was "too weak to walk and my nurse was unwilling, I walked five miles in the darkness in mud over my shoe tops, with my cheerful little baby in my arms," Mrs. Davis said. "There were various alarms of 'Yankees' at Frog Level and other places on the road, but about one o'clock we reached in safety a little church (Woodward Baptist Church—five miles south of Chester) in which the treasure guardians had taken refuge. A little bride who had accompanied her husband, who was with the bank treasure, told me kindly, 'We are lying on the floor, but have left the communion table for you out of respect, but the additional comfort of the table did not tempt one to commit sacrilege."[252]

Mrs. Davis, who was riding in an ambulance, took up quarters in the Woodward church with the other ladies. Parker, as commanding officer, slept in the pulpit while the midshipmen who were not on duty lay down under the trees outside in company with the mules.[253]

After a weary night they moved on at daybreak.

"We took up the line of march with the Charlotte company in advance and during the rest of the march the midshipmen led the advance one day and the Charlotte company the next, Parker said. "All hands were on foot, myself included, and I gave strict orders that no man should ride unless sick."[254]

Mrs. Davis said, "Captain Parker was exceedingly kind and attentive to us. We held no communications with the actual guardians of either the Confederate or bank treasury. The price for provisions on the road, from the hostelries and even the private houses, was fifty cents or one dollar for a biscuit, and the same for a glass of milk. It was difficult to feed my children except when we reached the house of some devoted Confederate, and then I did not like to avail of their generosity."[255]

About sunset of the first day's full day's march on April 14, they went into camp at Salem Crossroads, not far from Winnsboro in Fairfield County. While Parker was arranging a place for the ladies to sleep, he saw a man coming from a neighboring house.

"I found it was Mr. Edward C. Means who had been a midshipman with me in the USS Yorktown and who was then a Lieutenant in the Confederate Navy," Parker said. "He had lately had command of a gunboat on the James river. Means took all the ladies to his house and made them comfortable for the night. His plantation had fortunately escaped the ravages of General Sherman's army. Sherman's left wing had just cleared it but he told me he had only to go a few miles to see the ruins of many houses burned by Sherman's troops and most of them had been owned by his relatives. He was a descendant of Governor (John Hugh) Means. He showed me that night a trap door under his dining room table where a pit had been dug in which to conceal the family silver, etc."[256]

The little caravan started west very early the next morning on April 15 and about noon crossed the Broad river on a pontoon bridge. "I was surprised to see so beautiful a sheet of water," Parker said. "It reminded me of something I had read of General Sumter or Marion in the revolutionary war."[257]

Parker and his entourage marched 30 miles between their camp at Means' house at Salem Crossroads and Newberry, and as he had to be sometimes with the rear guard and at others in advance, he did more walking than anyone else.[258]

"The first night in camp I heard the midshipmen discussing the prospects of a long march and the probability of Old Parker's breaking down but I had walked too many midwatches to have any fears of it," Parker said. [259]

"I had an idea that naval officers should be good walkers," Parker said. "It was so in my case at least for upon our arrival at Washington, Georgia, I was almost the only officer who had not at some time during the march ridden in an ambulance or wagon. I did not have a blister on my feet during the whole time and found I could make my three miles an hour with great regularity and without discomfort."[260]

Still believing that Stoneman was in pursuit of them with his cavalry, Parker left rear guards at every bridge they crossed to be ready to burn it if necessary to check a pursuit. "I am not sure now whether General Stoneman ... was after us or not but we thought at the time he would get news of the treasure at Charlotte and follow us," Parker would write later.[261]

"During the march I never allowed any one to pass us on the road and yet the coming of the treasure was known at every village we passed through. How this should be was beyond my comprehension. I leave it to metaphysicians to solve as also the fact that when an army meets with a disaster, mysterious rumors are circulated concerning it before one would suppose sufficient time

The Burt-Stark House in Abbeville, S.C.
Photo by Pat McNeely

had elapsed for the news to travel the distance."[262] After marching twelve hours without stopping, they arrived at Newberry at 4 p.m. on April 17.[263]

Parker had sent a courier on ahead to ask the quartermaster to have a train of cars ready to take them on to Abbeville, South Carolina, which was 45 miles away.[264]

"Finally, when it seemed we had endured fatigue enough to have put a 'girdle round the earth,' more dead than alive, we reached Abbeville, arriving by April 19," Mrs. Davis said.[265] The train arrived at midnight and Parker and his men spent the night in the cars, and without halting, transferred the treasure to different rail cars and left the next evening at sunset for Washington, Georgia.[266] Mrs. Davis and her exhausted family went to the home of the Honorable Armistead Burt, a former

89

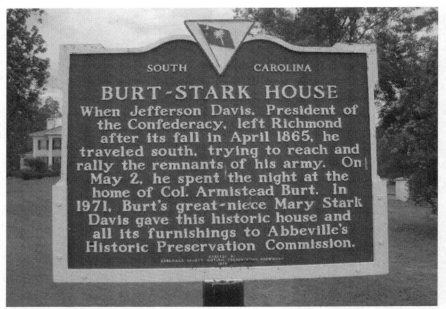

Marker at the Burt-Stark House in Abbeville, South Carolina
Photo by Pat McNeely

member of the U.S. Congress.[267] "Our welcome was as warm as though we had something to confer," Mrs. Davis said. "Mr. Armistead Burt and his wife received us in their fine house with a generous, tender welcome, thoughtfully expecting that, for having given us shelter, it would be burnt by the enemy. There we remained for a few days resting, and in painful expectation of worse news.

"It came, as we feared, all too soon."[268]

12 PRESIDENT LINCOLN'S ASSASSINATION

Even though President Lincoln said he didn't believe in dreams, he started having a recurring dream soon after the war began in 1861 that returned so often while he was in the White House that he came to regard it as a welcome visitor.[269]

"It was of a pleasing and promising character having nothing in it of the horrible," he told his friend Ward Hill Lamon. "It was always an omen of a Union victory and came with unerring certainty just before every military or naval engagement where our arms were crowned with success."[270]

In his dream Lincoln saw a badly damaged ship sailing away rapidly with their victorious vessels in close pursuit. He saw also the close of a battle on land, the enemy routed, and Federal forces in possession of vantage ground of incalculable importance.[271]

"Mr. Lincoln stated it as a fact that he had this dream just before the battles of Antietam, Gettysburg, and other signal engagements throughout the war," Lamon said.[272]

Although the dream that preceded Federal victories had been pleasant with projections of good news, by the end of March 1865, Lincoln began having a different dream—this time about assassination, according to Lamon, Lincoln's friend and biographer.[273]

Just three days before his assassination, Lincoln told Lamon and others about his new dream, saying:

"About ten days ago, I retired very late," Lincoln said. "I had been up waiting for important dispatches from the front. I could not have been long in bed when I fell into a slumber, for I was weary. I soon began to dream. There seemed to be a death-like stillness about me.[274]

"Then I heard subdued sobs, as if a number of people were weeping. I thought I left my bed and wandered down-

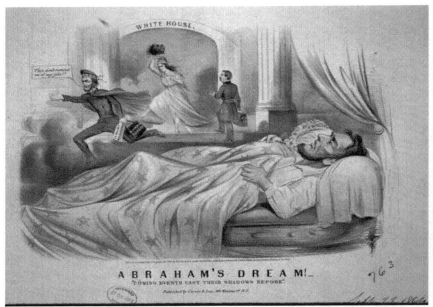

President Lincoln started having recurring dreams.
Source: Library of Congress

stairs. There the silence was broken by the same pitiful sobbing, but the mourners were invisible. I went from room to room; no living person was in sight, but the same mournful sounds of distress met me as I passed along. I saw light in all the rooms; every object was familiar to me; but where were all the people who were grieving as if their hearts would break? I was puzzled and alarmed. What could be the meaning of all this.[275]

"Determined to find the cause of a state of things so mysterious and so shocking, I kept on until I arrived at the East Room, which I entered. There I met with a sickening surprise. Before me was a catafalque, on which rested a corpse wrapped in funeral vestments. Around it were stationed soldiers who were acting as guards; and there was a throng of people, gazing mournfully upon the corpse, whose face was covered, others weeping pitifully.[276]

"'Who is dead in the White House?' I demanded of one of the soldiers, 'The President,' was his answer; 'he was killed by an assassin.' Then came a loud burst of grief from the crowd, which woke me from my dream. I slept no more that night; and although it was only a dream, I have been strangely annoyed by it ever since."[277]

Lincoln tried to brush off the dream, saying, "In this dream it was not me, but some other fellow, that was killed."

Mary Todd Lincoln
Source: Library of Congress

Someone else had been assassinated and not himself, he said.[278]

The last time Lincoln had the "good" dream that portended a Federal victory was the night before his assassinnation.[279]

"On the morning of that lamentable day, there was a Cabinet meeting at which General Grant was present," Lamon said. "During an interval of general discussion, the President asked General Grant if he had any news from General Sherman who was then confronting Johnston. The reply was in the negative but the general added that he was in hourly expectation of a dispatch announcing Johnston's surrender, Mr. Lincoln then with great impressiveness said, 'We shall hear very soon and the news will be important.' General Grant asked him why he thought so. 'Because , said Mr. Lincoln, 'I had a dream last night and ever since this war began I have had the same dream just before every event of great national importance. It portends some important event that will happen very soon.'"[280]

After that Lincoln became unusually cheerful. In the afternoon he ordered a carriage for a drive. Mrs. Lincoln asked him if he wished anyone to accompany them. "'No, Mary,' said he. 'I prefer that we ride by ourselves today. Mrs. Lincoln said afterwards that she never saw him look happier than he did during that drive."[281]

In reply to a remark of hers to that effect, Mr. Lincoln said, 'And well may I feel so, Mary, for I consider that this day the war has come to a close. Now we must try to be more cheerful in the future for between this terrible war and the loss of our darling son, we have suffered much misery. Let us both try to be happy."[282]

Lincoln's comments about his dreams—especially the assassination dream—were still on Mrs. Lincoln's mind on the night of April 14, when the President was shot at the Ford Theatre. Mrs. Lincoln's first exclamation was: "His dream was prophetic."[283]

Ford's Theatre in 1865. Source: Library of Congress

Lewis Payne, also known as Lewis Powell and Lewis Thornton Powell
Source: Library of Congress

While the Lincolns were making plans to attend "Our American Cousin" at Ford's Theatre on April 14, Sherman was receiving word that Major Robert Anderson would raise the Federal flag over Fort Sumter at noon that same day.[284]

Anderson had been the officer in charge when Fort Sumter was attacked almost exactly four years before on April 12, 1861.

And on the same day the flag was raised at Fort Sumter, Lewis Payne (or Powell), who was said to be working for the Confederate Secret Service in Maryland, arrived at the Herndon House in Washington, D.C., at 8 p.m., where John Wilkes Booth was giving out assignments to assassinate President Lincoln, Vice President Johnson, Seward, Grant and other members of the cabinet.[285] A carriage repair man, George Atzerodt said, "This is the way it came about: On the evening of the 14th of April I met Booth and Payne at the Herndon House in this city at 8 o'clock. He (Booth) said he himself would take care of

Mr. Lincoln and General Grant, (who he thought would be at the theater that night), Payne should take Mr. Seward, and I should take Mr. Johnson. I told him I would not do it; that I had gone into the thing to capture, but I was not going to kill.

George Atzerodt
Source: Library of Congress

He told me I was a fool; that I would be hung anyhow, and that it was death for every man that backed out, and so we parted."[286]

Even though Booth assigned Atzerodt to kill the Vice President at the Kirkwood Hotel, Atzerodt said he never tried but instead wandered the streets until about 2 a.m. that night. The next day he pawned his pistol at Georgetown before going to his cousin's house in Montgomery County, where he was arrested on April 19.[287]

Sam Arnold and Michael McLaughlin[288] were each assigned to kill cabinet officers but neither followed through on their assignments.

"General Grant did not go with Mr. Lincoln to the theater that night and thereby escaped," according to Jones.[289] Grant had at the last minute turned down an invitation to attend the theater that night, pleading that he had to visit his children.[290]

Booth's co-conspirators Lewis Payne and David Herold, who was unemployed except for a brief job clerking for a druggist, were assigned to kill Secretary of State William H. Seward. By simultaneously eliminating the top four people in the administration, Booth and his co-conspirators hoped to sever the continuity of the U.S. government. Payne said he was assigned to meet Booth at the Anacostia Bridge "after the deed was done."[291]

Major Henry Rathbone
Source: Library of Congress

John Edward Buckingham, who was the doorkeeper at Ford's Theater, re-membered that Booth came in and out of the theater five times before he finally committed the crime. "He was naturally a nervous man and restless in his movements," Buckingham said. "I can see that Booth must have been under great stress of excitement, although his actions did not seem to me at that time to be at all strange."[292]

Booth asked what time it was. "I told him to step into the lobby and there he could see the clock," Buckingham said. "Next he came and asked me to give him a chew of tobacco which I readily did. Afterwards I went into the saloon just below the theater to get a drink, and Booth was there drinking brandy."[293] Buckingham went back to the door and Booth soon returned. "He passed into the house and stood a moment looking at the audience and

Booth leaped from the President's Box and fled across the stage.
Source: Library of Congress

then went out again. Shortly afterwards he returned and passed in and around upstairs into the balcony humming a tune. I did not see where he went at the time for I was engaged in putting my checks in a little closet that I had there and was so occupied when I heard the pistol shot."[294]

Lincoln and his party were occupying two boxes at Ford's Theater, and the partition between them had been taken out so that it was one large box. In one compartment sat Lincoln and Clara Harris, the daughter of Senator Ira Harris of New York, and in the other were Mrs. Lincoln and Major Henry Rathbone,[295]a distant cousin of Actor Basil Rathbone. Harris was Rathbone's fiancé. The box was guarded by John Frederick Parker,[296] who left his post at intermission to join Lincoln's footman and carriage coachman for drinks in the Star Saloon next door to Ford's Theatre.[297] Parker had a history of misconduct and had been charged with dereliction of duty and conduct unbecoming an officer several times before that night.

When the second scene of the third act was being performed, Rathbone was watching the stage intently with his back toward the door when he heard a pistol discharged behind him. When he looked around, he saw a man through the smoke between the door and the President.[298]

At the same time Rathbone heard the man shout something that he thought sounded like "Freedom Thinks." Rathbone sprang toward him, but the man pulled away and stabbed at Rathbone with a large knife. Rathbone parried the blow with his left arm, which was cut several inches deep between his elbow and shoulder. When the assassin rushed to the front of the box, Rathbone tried to catch him again, but only ripped his clothes. Within 30 seconds after firing the shot, the assassin leaped over the railing of the box onto the stage, and Rathbone cried out with a loud voice, "Stop that man."[299] Buckingham turned just in time to see the assassin leap to the stage although for a moment he did not recognize the man as Booth. "It was only when he raised himself and gave utterance to the words *Sic Semper Tyrannis* (thus always to tyrants) that I discovered it was John Wilkes Booth," Buckingham said.[300]

"Those who were at the theater on that occasion will never forget the shock that for an instant paralyzed every energy in the vast audience as the sound of the shot fell upon ears and they saw a man then leap from the box in which the President was seated brandishing a long knife in his hand," Buckingham said. "As he struck the stage he hissed between clenched teeth the words *Sic Semper Tyrannis* and then, rushing back behind the scenes disappeared. It all happened in a moment."[301]

Those in the immediate front rows of the orchestra were the first to understand the crime that had been committed, and many rushed for the stage to try to capture or hold the assassin.[302]

George Alfred Townsend, a reporter for the *New York World,*[303] said William Withers, who was the leader of the orchestra, was the first to get within reaching distance of Booth, "who slashed Withers' dress coat across the sleeve and breast"[304] and fled.

Laura Keene was an actress in the play who climbed up the stage steps to cradle the dying President in her arms.
Source: Library of Congress

"The plans of the assassin had been too well laid," Townsend said. "He had his trained assistants in waiting....reached the alley in the rear, leaped upon his horse and fled across the Navy Yard bridge and rode rapidly away.[305]

"His horse's hoofs might almost have been heard amid the silence that for a few seconds dwelt in the interior of the theater. Then Mrs. Lincoln screamed, Miss Harris cried for water, and the full ghastly truth broke upon all. The President is murdered.[306] The scene that ensued was as tumultuous and terrible as one of Dante's pictures of hell. Some women fainted, others uttered piercing shrieks and cries for vengeance and unmeaning shouts for help burst from the mouths of men."[307]

Buckingham said, "No one can picture the horror and excitement that took possession of that audience. Everybody jumped to their feet. Ladies screamed and fainted. Men cried, 'Stop him' and several jumped to the stage in their effort to prevent Booth's escape."[308]

Ex-Mayor Richard Wallack, who was standing on the sidewalk in front of the theater, was called in to ask the people to leave. He begged them to leave as quietly and as speedily as possible, Buckingham said. "In this way the

The dying president was carried in the arms of friends to the Petersen House. *Source: Library of Congress.*

theater was emptied and then attention was turned to Mr. Lincoln whose head had fallen forward and who was evidently unconscious and breathing stertorously."[309]

The theater was immediately occupied by United States troops and a guard placed at every entrance.[310]

While the theatre was still in chaos, Rathbone was tending to the President whose position had not changed—the President's head was bent slightly forward and his eyes were closed. Rathbone saw that he was unconscious and supposing him mortally wounded rushed to the door to call for medical aid.[311] When Rathbone reached the outer door of the passage, he found it barred by a heavy piece of plank with one end secured in the wall and the other rested against the door. It had been fastened so securely that he had to use force to remove it. The guard who was supposed to be inside the passage was across the streeet at a tavern, which had given Booth the opportunity to slip inside the President's box and lock the

The Petersen house was across the street from Ford's Theater.
Source: Library of Congress

Friends and family gathered in the tiny bedroom of the Petersen house with the dying President. Source: Library of Congress

door behind him. This wedge or bar was about four feet from the floor, and people on the outside were pushing against the door to get in. When Rathbone removed the bar and opened the door, several people who said they were surgeons were allowed to enter, but Rathbone posted a guard to keep other people out of the box.[312]

Miss Laura Keene, an actress in the play, paused one moment before the footlights to entreat the audience to be calm before climbing the stairs in the rear of Lincoln's box. "(She) took the dying President's head in her lap, bathed it with the water she had brought and endeavoured to force some of the liquid through the insensible lips," Townsend said.[313] "The locality of the wound was at first supposed to be in the breast. It was not until after the neck and shoulders had been bared and no mark discovered that the dress of Miss Keene stained with blood revealed where the ball had penetrated."[314]When Rathbone returned to the box, he found the actress holding Lincoln's head in her lap while the physicians were examining him.[315] Within minutes, the decision was made to move Lincoln across the street to the house of German tailor William A. Petersen, where Lincoln would remain until he died the next morning. [316]

Surgeon General Dr. Joseph Barnes was quickly summoned.[317] As Lincoln's body was being carried out of the theatre, Rathbone asked Major Potter to help him assist the "intensely excited" Mrs. Lincoln across the street to the Petersen house.[318] By that time, Rathbone was bleeding so profusely from his own wounds that he fainted when he reached the house and was laid on the floor in the hall.[319] When he regained consciousness, he was taken in a carriage to his house.[320]

The room to which the President had been conveyed is on the first floor at the end of the hall and is only fifteen feet square with a Brussels carpet. A table and bureau spread with crochet work, eight chairs and the bed were all the furniture.

"Upon this bed, a low walnut four poster, lay the dying President, the blood oozing from the frightful wound in his head and staining the pillow," Townsend said. "All that the medical skill of half a dozen accomplished surgeons could do had been done to prolong a life evidently ebbing from a mortal hurt."[321]

13 THE ATTACK ON SECRETARY OF STATE SEWARD

John Wilkes Booth's conspiracy had embraced not only President Lincoln but also other members of his Cabinet. On the same night of April 14 that President Lincoln was assassinated, Lewis Payne (also known as Lewis Paine and Lewis Thornton Powell) attempted to kill Secretary of State William H. Seward in his house at Fifteen and a Half Street.[322]

Secretary of State William H. Seward
Source: Library of Congress

George Atzerodt, who was assigned to kill Vice President Andrew Johnson, had hidden a knife and pistol under the bed in a room that he had taken in the Kirkwood Hotel where President Johnson was staying. But Townsend said either Atzerodt's "courage failed or a trifling accident" derailed his plans, and he did not follow through on his assignment. Sam Arnold and Michael McLaughlin[323] were each assigned to kill a cabinet officer, but they "grew pigeon-livered and ran away," according to Townsend.[324]

However, Payne's attempt on the life of Secretary Seward was "perhaps as daring if not as dramatic as the assassination of the President," Townsend said. [325] "(Payne) was one of three Kentucky brothers, all outlaws" and had accompanied one of his brothers who was known to have been involved in a bank robbery at St. Albans, Vermont, Townsend said.[326] "This Payne, besides being positively identified as the assassin of the Sewards, had no friend nor haunts in Washington," Townsend said. "He was simply a dispatched murderer and after the night of the crime struck northward of the frontier instead of southward in the company of Booth."[327]

Secretary of State Seward's house.
Source: Library of Congress

At 9:20 p.m., just minutes before Booth fired a shot at the President, Payne, who was described as "tall, athletic and dressed in light coloured clothes" stepped down from a horse in front of Seward's three-story brick residence in Madison Place where the secretary was feeble and recovering from a serious carriage accident just nine days earlier that had left him close to death.[328]

Leaving his horse standing, Payne rang at the door and told the servant he wanted to see Seward, but the servant said Seward was ill and that no visitors were admitted.[329]

"But I am a messenger from Dr. Verdi, Mr. Seward's physician," Payne said. "I have a prescription which I must deliver to him myself." The servant was still reluctant but Payne pushed him aside and went upstairs towards Seward's room.[330]

He was about to enter when Seward's son, Frederick, appeared from an opposite doorway and asked what he was doing there. Payne told him the same thing he had told the servant below, but when Frederick refused to let him in,

Lewis Payne attacked Frederick Seward. *Source: Library of Congress*

Payne hit him across the forehead with the butt of a pistol. As Frederick fell, Major William Seward, another and younger son of the secretary, emerged from his father's room. Without a word Payne drew a knife and struck the major several blows while rushing into the chamber.[331]

"As he did so then after dealing the nurse (Private George F. Robinson) a horrible wound across the bowels, he sprang to the bed upon which the secretary lay, stabbing him once in the face and neck," Townsend said. "Mr. Seward arose convulsively and fell from the bed to the floor. Turning and brandishing his knife anew, the assassin fled from the room, cleared the prostrate form of Frederick Seward in the hall, descended the stairs in three leaps and was out of the door and upon his horse in an instant. It is stated by a person who saw him mount that although he leaped upon his horse with most unseemly haste, he trotted away around the corner of the block with circumspect deliberation."[332]

At about the same time, Surgeon General Barnes was playing whist at the house of his friend Chief Justice David Kellogg Cartter on H Street between Fifteenth Street and Vermont Avenue. A little before 10 o'clock a man rushed to the door saying that Surgeon General Barnes was wanted immediately at the Seward's home. The man said an intruder had attempted to kill Seward and had cut him severely on the face, arms and body with a knife. When Barnes and Cartter reached Seward's side they found him exhausted by the shock of Payne's attack and loss of blood.[333]

Barnes had nearly finished dressing Seward's wounds when a carriage drove up to the door, and the doorbell rang violently. Judge Cartter went to the door and found a messenger who told him that the President had been shot at Ford's Theater and that he had been sent to bring General Barnes to his bedside. The frightened messenger said Judge Cartter's servant had told him that

Seward had been "all cut to pieces and was dying."[334]

As Barnes and Cartter raced to the President's side, "the news spread through the capital as if borne on tongues of flame," Townsend said. Senator Charles Sumner, hearing the news at his residence, took a carriage and drove at a gallop to the White House to find that Lincoln's son, Robert, and other members of the household were still unaware of the attack. Both drove to Ford's Theater and went immediately to the President's bedside. Secretary of War Edwin Stanton and other members of the cabinet were at hand almost as soon.[335]

President Lincoln's son Robert.
Source: Library of Congress

Soon a vast crowd surging up Pennsylvania avenue toward Willard's Hotel cried, "The President is shot. President Lincoln is murdered." Another crowd sweeping down the avenue met the first with the tidings that Secretary Seward had been assassinated in his bed.[336]

109

"Instantly a wild apprehension of an organized conspiracy and of other murders took possession of the people," Townsend said. "The shout to arms was mingled with the expressions of sorrow and rage that everywhere filled the air. Where is General Grant or where is Secretary Stanton? Where are the rest of the cabinet broke from thousands of lips.

"A conflagration of fire is not half so terrible as was the conflagration of passion that rolled through the streets and houses of Washington that awful night."[337]

The Rev. Phineas D. Gurley
Source: Library of Congress

As the facts of both tragedies became generally known, crowds gathered around both the Petersen house and Seward's residence in such vast and tumultous numbers that military guards could barely keep them away from the doors.[338]

All through the night while the horror-stricken crowds outside wept and gathered along the streets, the military and police were patrolling and weaving a cordon around the city while men were arming and asking each other, "What victim next?" [339]

While the telegraph was sending news from city to city over the continent and while the two assassins were speeding away on waiting horses, Lincoln's family and friends gathered and watched around his deathbed.

Occasionally he was visited by Dr. Phineas D. Gurley, pastor of the New York Avenue Presbyterian Church near the White House where Lincoln frequently prayed. Occasionally Mrs. Lincoln and her sons entered to find no hope and went back to ceaseless weeping.[340]

Members of the cabinet, senators, representatives, generals, and others took turns at the bedside. Chief Justice Salmon P. Chase remained until a late hour and returned in the morning. Secretary of the Treasury Hugh McCulloch remained a constant watcher until 5 a.m. in the morning.[341]

Senator Charles Sumner
Source: Library of Congress

Secretary of War Stanton and Secretary of the Navy Gideon Welles were already at Lincoln's side when Surgeon General Joseph Barnes arrived and took a seat beside the President to examine the wound caused by the pistol bullet. He carefully and tenderly noted where the entrance had been made and the probable course of the ball.[342] "The bullet had gone through one of the cervical vertebra and lodged in the brain," Buckingham said.

[343]When Stanton asked Barnes about Lincoln's condition, the doctor said, "'I fear, Mr Stanton, that there is no hope.' 'Oh no, general, no, no,'" and "the man of all others apparently strange to tears sank down beside the bed, the hot bitter evidences of an awful sorrow trickling through his fingers to the floor," Townsend said.[344]

Mary Todd Lincoln *Source: Library of Congress*

Senator Sumner sat on the opposite side of the bed holding one of the President's hands in his own and sobbing with kindred grief. Secretary (of the Navy Gideon) Welles stood at the foot of the bed, his frame shaken with emotion."345 Barnes shook his head gravely and announced that the wound was fatal and that death was a question of only a few hours.[346] The pronouncement confirmed the sad forebodings of Lincoln's two trusted secretaries Stanton and Welles, as well as Robert Lincoln, the President's oldest son, who had reached his father's bedside and was anxiously watching Barnes.[347]

"Mrs. Lincoln, who was prostrated with grief and wholly overcome by the shock of the tragedy, was in another room when she learned that there was no hope," Buckingham said.[348] Elizabeth Dixon, the wife of Senator James Dixon of Connecticut, soon arrived to stay with Mrs. Lincoln through the night.[349]

James Tanner, a disabled soldier who was a War Department clerk, lived in the house next door to the Petersen house. He had been watching the arrival of Washington's leaders and heard the news that Lincoln's condition was hopeless. Tanner was summoned to the house that night because of his shorthand skills when Secretary of War Stanton decided to take testimony about the shooting.[350]

"Mrs. Lincoln was in the front room, weeping as though her heart would break," Tanner said. "In the back room lay His Excellency breathing hard, and with every breath a groan."[351]

In the room were Vice President Andrew Johnson, all members of the Cabinet except Seward, several generals, Chief Justice Salmon P. Chase, Chief Justice Cartter and "many other distinguished men," Tanner said.[352] "A solemn silence pervaded the whole throng. It was a terrible moment."[353]

Tanner was put to work at about midnight. "Opposite me, at the table where I sat writing, sat Secretary Stanton writing despatches to General (John Adams) Dix and others, and giving orders for the guarding of Ford's and the surrounding country. At the left of me was Judge Cartter propounding the questions to the witnesses, whose answers I was jotting in Standard Phonography."[354]

"In fifteen minutes I had testimony enough down to hang Wilkes Booth, the assassin, higher than ever Haman hung. I was writing short hand for about an hour and a half when I commenced writing it out. I thought I had been writing about two hours, when I looked at the clock and it marked half past four A.M. I commenced writing about" midnight, Tanner later reported.[355]

"In the front room Mrs. Lincoln was uttering the most heartbroken exclamations all the night long," Tanner said. "As she passed through the hall back to the parlor after she had to take leave of the President for the last time—as she went by my door, I heard her moan, 'Oh, My God, and have I given my husband to die?' and I tell you, I never heard so much agony in so few words. The President was still alive but sinking fast."[356]

Tanner said the President had been "utterly unconscious from the time the shot struck him and remained so until he breathed his last." [357]

At 6:45 a.m. Saturday, Tanner finished his notes and passed into the back room where the President lay. "It was very evident that he could not last long," Tanner said.[358]

"There was quite a crowd in the room, which was small, but I approached quite near the bed on which so much greatness lay, fast losing its hold on this world. The head of the bed was towards the door.

"At the head stood Captain Robert Lincoln, weeping on the shoulder of Senator (Charles) Sumner. General (Henry) Halleck stood just behind Robert Lincoln and I stood just to the left of General Halleck and between him, and General [Montgomery Meigs]. Stanton was there, trying every way to be calm and yet he was very much moved.

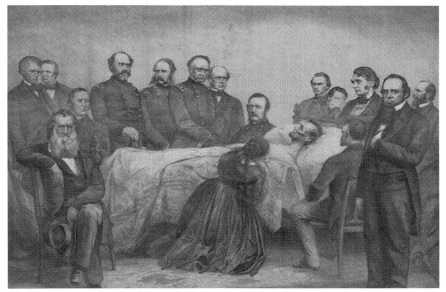

The last moments of President Lincoln's life. Source: Library of Congress

"The utmost silence pervaded, broken only by the sounds of strong men's tears," Tanner said.[359] The President breathed heavily until a few minutes before he breathed his last, then his breath came easily…. and he passed off very quietly."[360][361]

"Not a gleam of consciousness shone across the visage of the President up to his death, a quiet peaceful death at last which came at twenty two minutes past seven a. m." on April 15, Townsend said.[362]

The Rev. Dr. Gurley knelt with all around in prayer and then entered the adjoining room where were gathered Mrs. Lincoln, Captain Robert Lincoln, John Hay and others and prayed again.[363] Soon after 9 o'clock that morning, Lincoln's remains were placed in a temporary coffin and taken to the White House under a small escort.[364] Across town in Secretary Seward's chamber, visitors had also been alternating in and out of the bedroom through the night. It had been determined early

115

that the secretary's wounds were not likely to be fatal. A wire instrument to relieve the pain from previous injuries in a carriage accident prevented the assassin's knife from striking too deep. Frederick Seward's injuries were more serious. His forehead was broken in by the blow from the pistol, and he was still unconscious when the doctors arrived.[365]

Seward, who was unable to speak because of his injuries, was not told about the assassination of the President and the attack on his son until the next day, Townsend said.

"He had been worrying as to why Mr. Lincoln did not visit him. Why doesn't the President come to see me, he asked with his pencil. Where is Frederick? What is the matter with him? Perceiving the nervous excitement which these doubts occasioned, a consultation was had at which it was finally determined that it would be best to let the secretary know the worst. Secretary Stanton was chosen to tell him."

Sitting down beside Seward's bed, Stanton gave him a full account of the whole affair. "Mr. Seward was so surprised and shocked that he raised one hand involuntarily and groaned," Townsend said. "Such is the condition of affairs at this stage of the terror."[366]

Around the city, the pursuit of the assassins began. "The town is full of wild and baseless rumors," Townsend said. "Much that is said is stirring. Little is reliable. I tell it to you as I get it but fancy is more prolific than truth."[367]

14 JOHNSON SURRENDERS TO SHERMAN

Unaware that President Lincoln had died from an assassin's bullet at the Petersen House in Washington, D.C., and that Vice President Andrew Johnson had taken the oath of office early on the morning of April 15, General Sherman

Vice President Andrew Johnson was sworn in as president at 10 a.m. on April 15 in the small parlor of the Kirkwood Hotel in Washington, D.C. *Source: Library of Congress*

made plans to meet with General Johnston the next day at a point midway between Durham and the rear of Johnston's army near Hillsboro, North Carolina.

As Sherman was preparing to board the train for Durham, a telegraph operator arrived asking him to wait for transmission of an important dispatch in cipher from Morehead City.[368] "I held the train for nearly half an hour,

The surrender took place at the James Bennett home, which is a state park near Durham, North Carolina. *Photo by Pat McNeely*

when he returned with the message translated and written out," Sherman said. "It was from Mr. Stanton, announcing the assassination of Mr. Lincoln, the attempt on the life of Mr. Seward and son, and a suspicion that a like fate was designed for General Grant and all the principal officers of the Government. Dreading the effect of such a message at that critical instant of time, I asked the operator if any one besides himself had seen it; he answered No!" Sherman asked him not to reveal the contents until he returned that afternoon.[369]

Sherman reached Durham, which was 26 miles away, and rode up Hillsborough road for about five miles to the farmhouse of James Bennett to begin negotiating the surrender from Johnston. When the two generals were alone, Sherman showed Johnston the dispatch about Lincoln's assassination and watched him closely.

"The perspiration came out in large drops on his forehead, and he did not attempt to conceal his distress," Sherman said. "He denounced the act as a disgrace to the age, and hoped I did not charge it to the Confederate Government. I told him I could not believe that he or General Lee, or the officers of the Confederate army, could possibly be privy to acts of assassination; but I would not say as much for Jeff. Davis, George Sanders and men of that stripe."[370]

Sherman said that he dreaded the effect the news would have on his soldiers. "I feared some foolish woman or man in Raleigh might say something or do something that would madden our men, and that a fate worse than that of Columbia would befall the place."[371]

As soon as Sherman reached Raleigh, he published orders for the army and announced the assassination of President Lincoln.

"I doubt if, in the whole land, there were more sincere mourners over his sad fate than were then in and about Raleigh. I watched the effect closely, and was gratified that there was no single act of retaliation; though I saw and felt that one single word by me would have laid the city in ashes, and turned its whole population houseless upon the country, if not worse.[372]

The news of President Lincoln's death produced a "most intense effect" on Sherman's troops. "At first I feared it would lead to excess; but now it has softened down, and can easily be guided," Sherman said. "None evince more feeling than General Johnston, who admitted that the act was calculated to stain his cause with a dark hue; and he contended that the loss was most serious to the South, who had begun to realize that Mr. Lincoln was the best friend they had."[373]

Fearing that the Confederates would disperse and begin guerrilla warfare, Sherman was eager to come to an agreement with Johnston. Sherman and his generals wanted to end the war and dreaded the possibility of a long and harassing march in pursuit of a dissolving and fleeing army — "a march," he said, "that might carry us back again over the thousand miles that we had just accomplished....

"We discussed all the probabilities, among which was, whether, if Johnston made a point of it, I should assent to the escape from the country of Jeff. Davis and his fugitive cabinet; and some one of my general officers, either Logan or Blair, insisted that, if asked for, we should even provide a vessel to carry them to Nassau from Charleston."[374]

As Sherman began meeting with the Confederate generals, he was unaware of orders that had been issued on March 3 forbidding Grant (and thus any of his subordinates) from any conferences with Lee (and thus

General Johnston (right) disobeyed direct orders from President Davis and surrendered to General Sherman near Durham, N.C.
Source: Library of Congress

any of his subordinates), and Sherman assumed that he had the right to negotiate proposed terms of surrender for submission to President Andrew Johnson.[375]

"The President directs me to say to you that he wishes you to have no conference with General Lee unless it be for the capitulation of Lee's army or on some minor and purely military matter," Stanton had written to Grant in March. "He instructs me to say that you are not to decide, discuss, or confer on any political questions. The President, holding the decision of these questions in his own hands, will submit them to no military conference or convention. In the mean time you are to press to the utmost of your ability your military advantage."[376]

Unaware of the Presidential directive that had been sent to Grant but recalling his conversation with President Lincoln at City Point, Sherman wrote terms of surrender to submit to President Johnson. When Johnston asked about the political rights of his men and officers after the surrender, Sherman said that "Mr. Lincoln's proclamation of amnesty, of December 8, 1863, (was) still in force." The proclamation enabled every Confederate soldier and officer below the rank of colonel to obtain an absolute pardon by simply laying down his arms and taking the common oath of allegiance. "General Grant, in accepting the surrender of General Lee's army, had extended the same principle to all the officers, General Lee included; such a pardon, I understood, would restore to them all their rights of citizenship."[377]

While Sherman was preparing the proposed terms of surrender, Grant arrived in Raleigh and advised Sherman to accept Johnston's surrender on the same terms as his with Lee. So Sherman rode out to Bennett's house where he and Johnston signed the agreement on April 18. The agreement provided for the end of all acts of war and the surrender of all arms and public property and agreement for all offices and men to agree in writing not to take up arms against the U.S. government. Officers could keep side arms, and they would be permitted to keep private horses and baggage and return home.[378]

The agreement provided for the Confederate armies to disband and deposit their arms and public property in the State Arsenal and for each officer and man to file an agreement to cease from acts of war.[379]

While Confederate government officials were passing through North Carolina and Sherman and Johnston were negotiating, the body of Abraham Lincoln lay in state in the East Room before being moved to the Capitol Rotunda from April 19 through April 21.[380] For the final journey with his son Willie, both caskets were transported in the executive coach "United States," and for three weeks the Lincoln funeral train decorated in black bunting chugged slowly across the country from Washington, D.C., to Springfield, Illinois. The train stopped at cities along the way for large-scale memorials attended by thousands of mourners.[381]

Sherman thought often of Lincoln's words of praise and final advice at City Point and felt supremely satisfied with the results of his campaign through Georgia and the Carolinas. He knew how pleased Lincoln would have been with the impending surrender of the Confederate troops from Sherman's battlefields. Sherman ordered his troops to remain where they were with the cavalry occupying Durham's Station and Chapel Hill, General Henry Slocum's army at Aven's Ferry on Cape Fear River, General Oliver Howard's men strung out along the railroad toward Hillsboro, and the rest of the army in Raleigh.[382]

15 JEFFERSON DAVIS REACHES SOUTH CAROLINA

When General P.G.T. Beauregard reached Charlotte in late March, he issued orders to fortify the railroad bridge at Nation's Ford that crossed the Catawba River near the South Carolina border. It was near the spot where President Davis and his escort would cross in a few weeks.[383]

While Beauregard was arriving in Charlotte, General Stoneman's cavalry left Greenville in East Tenn-essee on an expedition to destroy the railroads and Lee's supply lines from North Carolina into Virginia.

General P.G.T. Beauregard Source: National Archives and Records Administration

Frank H. Mason was captain of the Twelfth Ohio Volunteer Cavalry under Stoneman's command as they marched into North Carolina on March 20. He said the plan and purpose of Stoneman's campaign had been kept so absolutely secret that not even the brigade commanders knew their destination or which enemy they were going to fight.[384]

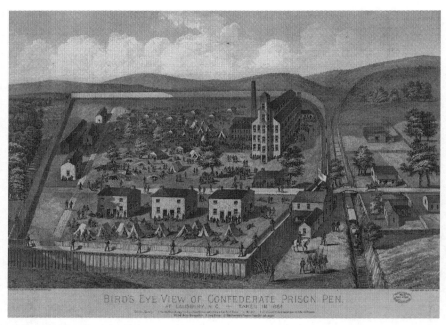

Bird's Eye View of the Confederate Prison Pen at Salisbury, N.C., taken in 1864. Source: Library of Congress Geography and Map Division.

After raiding Boone and Wilkesboro, Stoneman headed north toward Virginia, which caused a change in the defenses of the North Carolina Confederates. Beauregard, who was Johnston's commander in western North Carolina, was confused by Stoneman's maneuvers and thought that Greensboro and Danville were to be targets up until the time Stoneman approached Salisbury, North Carolina, 42 miles north of Charlotte, with the intention of confiscating everything possible and destroying what was left of the massive stores and munitions in Salisbury.[385]

Salisbury was a rich and important supply line for Lee's forces. The city held vast stores of ammunition, arms, provisions, medical and quartermaster's stores and factories for the manufacture of cloth for military clothing and was the home of a Confederate prisoner-of-war camp that the Federals intended to empty and destroy.[386]

Confederate troops that had been sent to defend Salisbury had been moved out to cover Greensboro and Danville, but by the time Davis reached Greensboro, Stoneman's cavalry had destroyed the rail from Lexington to Salisbury.[387]

Regiments were detailed to destroy the railway buildings and machinery and break up the track and bridges several miles to the south.[388] A strong detachment was sent out to capture the long railroad bridge over the Yadkin River, about six miles above town, but they were driven back by strong artillery fire and left the long bridge intact.

On the day that Salisbury fell, Beauregard ordered 1,000 soldiers to the site, but they arrived too late. After a 20-minute battle on April 12 on Grant Creek four or five miles from Salisbury, the Confederates fell back along the line, and Stoneman's troops closed in on the town, which fell without further resistance.[389]

"A detachment of six hundred men under Major Barnes was detailed to destroy Confederate property," Mason said. Most of the Union prisoners in the prisoner-of-war camp had been exchanged two months before or transferred to other prisons as Stoneman's column approached, and most of the prison was burned immediately.[390]

"Their work was prompt and thorough," Mason said, and included a 10,000-stand of small arms, 1 million pounds of musketry ammunition, 10,000 pounds of artillery cartridges and shells, 6,000 pounds of powder, 3 magazines, 10,000 bushels of corn, 6 depot buildings, 75,000 suits of uniform clothing, several thousand bales of cotton, 250,000 English army blankets, 20,000 pounds of leather, 100,000 pounds of salt, 10,000 pounds of saltpeter, 27,000 pounds of rice, 50,000 bushels of wheat, and an immense quantity of medical supplies, mostly imported.[391] "Fifteen millions of Confederate money were among the trophies," Mason said.[392] And "for the first time since leaving Tennessee, Stoneman's men and horses reveled in full rations. All that they could not use was put to the torch."[393]

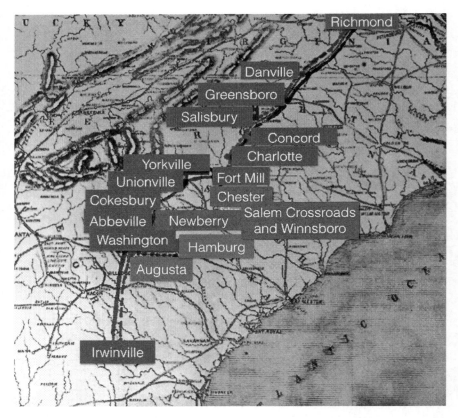

Varina Howell Davis left Richmond March 31. The President left Richmond April 2 and was followed later that night by the train carrying the gold from the Richmond banks and the Confederate treasury. Source: Library of Congress: Adapted by Pat McNeely

16 NEWS SPREADS ABOUT THE ASSASSINATION

Confederates and Federals knew the value of the Piedmont, Danville and Richmond Railway, which had been destroyed by General Stoneman's cavalry by the time he reached Salisbury, North Carolina. These were the last sections of the railroads that would otherwise have left an open door for General Lee's escape. The destruction of the rails in North and South Carolina had strangled the supply line for the military power of the Confederacy and had been part of the reason Lee had been forced to surrender on April 9.[394]

His mission accomplished, General Stoneman headed west toward Tennessee on April 17, while two of his brigades marched toward Knoxville.[395] If Stoneman had waited a few more hours to leave, President Davis, whose entourage was riding south in wagons and on horseback from Greensboro, would have ridden into Stoneman's arms in Salisbury.[396] By the time Davis reached Salisbury, the city was still smoldering, and no one offered him a place to stay. He was finally taken in by Thomas G. Haughton, rector of St. Luke's Episcopal Church.

General William J. Palmer's brigade stayed 25 miles from Charlotte at Dallas for several days where a battalion of the Twelfth Ohio, under Major Herrick, was sent to hold the Tuckasegee Ford on the Catawba River. There, Federals prevented the crossing of a brigade of General Joe Wheeler's cavalry, which they would learn later, formed part of President Davis' escort.[397]

Unaware that Davis was nearby and with no orders to arrest him, Stoneman and most of his command, along with Confederate prisoners, continued west. Another brigade under Palmer headed toward Davidson and

General Stoneman (standing center) and staff early in the war.
Source: Library of Congress

Lincolnton to destroy several railway bridges on the lines converging from the south on Charlotte.

Fearing the arrival of Stoneman's cavalry who were almost on their doorstep a few miles north of the city, directors at the Charlotte branch of the Bank of North Carolina, which was locally called the Dewey Bank, hurriedly made plans to hide the quarter of a million dollars in gold and coin that was being held in their vaults. The directors loaded the bank's assets at 122 South Tryon Street onto a wagon during the night and headed out Lawyer's Road. Finding a stream in a wooded glen that they called Grasshopper Springs, they sank the kegs of silver into stump holes where trees had once burned and dug holes and buried the larger boxes of gold.[398]

While Davis was riding out of Salisbury toward Charlotte, Major E.C. Moderwell with 200 men from the Twelfth Ohio, were sent on a raid to destroy the 1,100-foot bridge on the Charlotte and South Carolina Railroad over the Catawba River. Unaware that Davis was arriving in Charlotte, the Federal raiders skirmished that day with

Catawba Bridge near Nation's Ford was burned by the Federals.
Source: Benson J. Lossing, Pictorial History of the Civil War, (Hartford: Belknap, 1868)

Confederates for two hours and burned the bridge after skirting around Charlotte and into South Carolina.[399] It was the same bridge that Beauregard had fortified when he first arrived in town and was near Nation's Ford where Davis would cross into South Carolina near Rock Hill a few days later on April 26.[400]

After the last of Stoneman's men marched all night to rejoin their brigade at Dallas, North Carolina, President Davis and his entourage of a thousand cavalry arrived in Charlotte on April 19 to be greeted by enthusiastic crowds.[401] Davis stood on the southwest corner of South Tryon and Fourth streets to make a speech of gratitude.[402]

Soon after Davis arrived, he received a telegram announcing the assassination of President Lincoln, but it was not believed.[403] When General John Breckinridge arrived on the train that afternoon, he went immediately to see the President. After shaking hands, Davis asked: "Is it true, General, that Mr. Lincoln was killed?" "Yes, sir," said Breckinridge, who had just come from the front. "General Sherman received a telegram this morning that he was shot in Ford's theatre, at Washington, last night."[404]

Davis said promptly and with feeling, "I am sorry to learn it. Mr. Lincoln was a much better man than his successor will be, and it will go harder with our people. It is bad news for us."[405]

News was so slow reaching Davis in Charlotte that he did not know that funeral services for President Lincoln were being held that day in the East Room of the White House. After brief services, the funeral carriage, with a military escort and bands playing sorrowful dirges, carried the body past throngs of people to the rotunda of the Capitol, where it would remain until April 20.[406]

Unaware of the funeral, Davis told Breckinridge that he had notified General Johnston that he approved of his last action, but in doing so he doubted whether the agreement would be ratified by the United States Government.[407]

"The opinion entertained in regard to President Johnson and Stanton, his venomous Secretary of War, did not permit me to expect that they would be less vindictive after a surrender of our army had been proposed than when it was regarded as a formidable body in the field," Davis said. [408]

17 GENERAL SMITH DEVELOPS THE TRANS-MISSISSIPPI

General Edmund Kirby Smith was 37 years old when he was sent west to command the Army of East Tennessee. Tall with slightly graying black hair, black beard and mustache, he had taught math at West Point before the war.[409]

He had scored a victory at the Battle of Richmond, Kentucky, where his troops had forced the Federals to retreat toward Louisville on August 30, 1862. Although Smith preferred active service in the field, he was appointed

General Edmund Kirby Smith
Source: Library of Congress

in February 1863 to command the Confederate forces west of the Mississippi.[410] And, in May 1863, he moved his headquarters to Shreveport, Louisiana, where he took command of the Trans-Mississippi Department, which included Texas, Louisiana, Arkansas, Missouri and vast Indian territories.[411] He set up residence at 912 Commerce Street in Shreveport, where he lived until the Confederacy fell in 1865.[412]

He began organizing a government that was so successful that the Confederacy established a Post Office

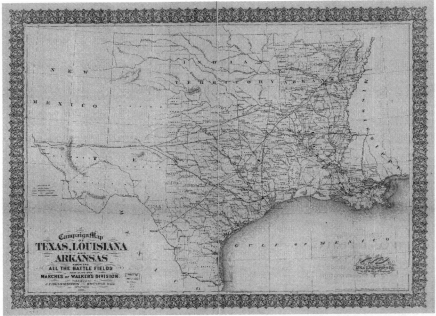

The Trans-Mississippi Empire included Texas, Louisiana, Arkansas, Missouri and vast Indian territories. Source: Library of Congress, Geography and Map Division

Department and a branch of the Treasury Department there. However, after the surrender of Vicksburg, the Federal Army took control of the Mississippi River, which cut off the Trans-Mississippi Department from the Confederate States of the East.[413]

The transfer of troops, or even of orders, became so difficult that President Davis verbally ordered him to exercise civil as well as military authority. When Kirby resisted, saying there was no constitutional authority for those powers, Davis said that the "exigencies of the case demanded it and were superior to all law."[414]

Thus, with full control and unlimited command over the vast territory west of the Mississippi River, Smith reorganized the Department, gathered the scattered

Federal guns fire on a Confederate ship running the blockade.
Source: Library of Congress

forces, and established a strong central government that would come to be known as "KirbySmithdom." He called together the governors of the states, Supreme Court judges and other officials, and on August 18, 1863, the Governors united in an "Address to the People of Texas, Louisiana, Arkansas and Missouri, and the Allied Indian Nations," in which they unanimously and with full confidence and trust in Smith "sustained the vigorous and decided policy he proposed to pursue."[415]

The General studied economic conditions in the Trans-Mississippi Department by gathering inventories of the resources of the country—mineral, agricultural and manufacturing—and using the information effectively. Even though he was blocked by Federal forces that controlled the Mississippi River, he began communicating with Confederate officials by running the blockade at Galveston, Texas, and Wilmington, North Carolina.[416] He sent large quantities of cotton to Confederate agents abroad, imported machinery from Europe, established factories and machine shops and salt works and manufactured and traded with England. He made the Department the only really productive portion of the Confederacy.[417]

Since the newly formed Confederacy was not officially recognized by the various foreign powers, the seceded states sought the aid of various shipping companies and other businesses to sell and ship the much needed supplies and ordnance to the Confederacy.[418]

To handle its important business transactions, the Confederate government had chosen John Fraser & Company, a Charleston-based importing and exporting company that was well connected in Europe and became an unofficial arm of the Confederate government. Established in 1835, John Fraser, Sr., had turned the business over to his son, John Augustus Fraser, and his senior partner, George A. Trenholm, who was one of the wealthiest men in the south when the war began and would become Confederate Secretary of the Treasury in 1864.[419]

By 1860 the company had five seagoing vessels making shipping runs from Liverpool, England, to New York and Charleston. Even before the first battles began, Fraser & Company had already begun negotiations for steamship service between England and points along the southern coast of the Confederacy. Taking advantage of the fact that neither side was fully prepared for war, Trenholm and his partners began shipping arms from Liverpool and New York to Charleston. The seceded state of South Carolina bought the first shipments and sold them to the Confederate government. As soon as other southern states seceded from the Union, nearly all of Trenholm's business was with the Confederacy.[420]

Ashley Hall, a private school at 172 Rutledge Avenue in Charleston, S.C., was one of the primary residences of George A. Trenholm during the Civil War. Source: Library of Congress

Another affiliated company, Fraser, Trenholm and Company was the English branch of Fraser and Company, based in Charleston.[421] Fraser, Trenholm became a depository of Confederate funds, asking a commission of ½ percent, which was the same rate believed paid to Baring Brothers, a British merchant bank used by the United States for similar services.[422]

The English branch of John Fraser & Co. at

10 Rumford Place in Liverpool, England, became the common connection for the Confederacy's naval and financial dealings in Europe and ran a fleet of ships through the Federal blockade. By June 1861, when $500,000 was placed to the credit of Fraser, Trenholm in Liverpool, the company had become a branch of the Confederate Treasury.[423] The firm's senior partner in Liverpool, Charles K. Prioleau, was a naturalized Englishman, who had been brought up in Charleston, South Carolina, where most of his family still lived.[424]

Fraser, Trenholm not only supplied the credit to maintain the Confederacy but was responsible for most of the trade between England and the South. It was actively engaged in blockade running, financing the supply of armaments, organizing the building of ships and commerce destroyers, assisting in acquiring Confederate loans and constantly lobbying European parliaments.[425]

And after the General took over the Trans-Mississippi Department, his Cotton Bureau was sending a constant stream of cotton and other commodities through the Liverpool office. Even though Texas was a significant cotton-producing State, her navigable rivers were not available for trade and there were few railroads. So cotton was hauled on wagons for great distances over the plains —four hundred miles in some instances—to Brownsville, where it was exported.[426]

Through the Bureau, the General bought cotton at three and four cents a pound and sold it at fifty cents a pound in gold, and it passed in constant streams, in defiance of blockades, to the agents of the Department abroad.[427] It is estimated that in 1863-64 more than 500,000 bales of cotton reached Europe by these means.[428] Texas had escaped the destruction that fell on the other States of the Confederacy and, in addition to the vast crops of cotton being exported to Europe and Mexico, their crops of grain were the largest they had ever seen.

The state was able to supply adjacent parts of the country with grain, beef and mutton. Smith's success in the Trans-Mississippi Department demonstrated to the Federals the importance of the possession of the Mississippi River.[429]

While becoming an economic power, the Trans-Mississippi Department was not wholly withdrawn from the war. They were engaged in the defense of the Red River and celebrated the repulse of the Federal invasion at Sabine Pass, Texas, on September 8, 1863,[430] but most of Smith's time was taken up with development of the vast resources available in his territory.

As bad news drifted west of the Mississippi during February 1865, Smith began negotiating with Emperor Maximilian for the transfer of his troops to Mexico. The sympathy of the Maximilian regime for the

Emperor Maximilian of Mexico Source: Library of Congress

Confederate States was well known, and as the Confederacy fell to pieces, some of the leaders, especially those in the Southwest, began making plans to seek personal asylum in the Mexican Empire.[431]

Although President Davis never intended to seek refuge in Mexico, he was moving southwest through the Carolinas and Georgia in an effort to reach "KirbySmithdom," where Davis believed the war could be continued indefinitely with an alliance with Mexico.[432]

Smith wrote letters in February to a Mexican official[433], who had, sometime before the war, been connected with the United States Government in a diplomatic capacity.[434] Smith said, "I desire you, on some fitting occasion, to make known to His Majesty, the Emperor, that in case of unexampled catastrophe to our arms and the final overthrow of the government which I have the honor to represent as the Military Chief of the States West of the Mississippi River—an event I do not now apprehend, but which yet may possibly occur in the future, it is my fixed purpose to leave my native land and seek an asylum in Mexico."[435] In a letter, he described his military education and background and said that he wanted to continue with his military career.[436]

"Having some knowledge of the French and Spanish languages and having been on duty at one period on the Mexican Frontier, my humble services and such influence as I could exert might be rendered available to His Majesty's Government," he wrote. "I therefore authorize you to tender them to him in the possibility of the contingency above alluded to."[437]

He said that "the natural antipathy to the North in the minds of many citizens of the Confederate States together with their intelligence, endurance and daring as soldiers, might, in contemplation of possible collision between the

Imperial Government and the United States of the North, render very desirable such a corps of Southern soldiers as might be induced by the offer of liberal terms to colonize the Empire and thus greatly strengthen it."[438]

Smith said, "Should you find that this offer and the accompanying views are not wholly inappropriate to be alluded to, you will please tender my services to the Emperor and at the same time assure him of my heartfelt wish for the eminent success of his reign and the honor, welfare and happiness of his people."[439]

Smith wrote to the diplomat again with even greater urgency on May 2.[440] "Having entire confidence in your patriotism and experience, I have deemed you a suitable person to present to His Majesty the Emperor certain views as to the future interest of the Confederate States and the Empire of Mexico."[441]

He said as the Military Commander of the Department, he had no authority to appoint diplomatic agents or to initiate negotiations with foreign powers.[442] "Yet in the present condition of our national affairs, I deem it highly important from a military point of view, at least, to place myself in communication with the Government of Mexico," he said.

"While, therefore, you will expressly disclaim any authority from the Confederate Government to act in a diplomatic capacity, you may give assurances that there is every probability that our Government will be willing to enter into a liberal agreement with the authorities of the Mexican Empire based upon the principle of mutual protection from their common enemy."[443]

He said he could not disguise the fact that recent reverses of the most serious character had befallen the Confederate arms.

"Nor can it be denied that there is a probability of still further losses to us," he said. "It may even be that it is the inscrutable design of Him who rules the destinies of nations that the day of our ultimate redemption should be postponed. If then, final catastrophe should overwhelm our just cause, the contiguity of Mexico to us and the future designs of the United States must naturally be a subject of the deepest solicitude to His Imperial Majesty."[444]

He warned of impending aggression toward Mexico by the United States government. "From the solemn action of their Houses of Congress, from the public expressions of eminent persons standing high in the confidence of both the civil and military authorities of the United States, from the tone of their public journals, which have hitherto rarely failed to foreshadow the policy of that Government, it is plain that further schemes of ambition and of territorial aggrandizement are being nursed and matured by the United States," he said.[445]

"It is equally clear, judging by the signs of the times, that they look with jealous eyes upon the neighboring Empire of Mexico, and that they meditate a blow aimed at its destruction. Your own information on these points will enable you to expose more fully the ambitious designs of our enemy in that quarter.[446]

"If such be the ultimate purpose of the Federal Government, it cannot fail to strike His Imperial Highness that in the Confederate States, and more especially in the Department adjoining his dominions, and over which I have the honor to preside as Military Chief, there are many trained soldiers inured to the hardships of the field and inspired with a bitter hatred of the Federals, whose services might be tendered to him against the North."[447]

Smith explained that he had under his command

60,000 men, including 9,000 Missourians who had been driven from their homes, who would look favorably on immigration and protection and who would take service with the power favoring them.[448]

"There are, besides, no less than 10,000 men, daring and gallant spirits from other States, in this Department, to whom a state of vassalage to the Federal Government would be intolerable and who would gladly rally around any flag that promised to lead them to battle against their former foe," he said.

"These men are commanded by veteran officers who have repeatedly led them in action and who thoroughly understand their character and could control them without difficulty."[449]

"If I am not mistaken in my conclusion as to the future policy of the United States, the propriety of an understanding between the Emperor and the Confederate States Government for their mutual defence (sic) will be apparent to His Majesty. The services of our troops would be of inestimable value to him," he said, asking the emissary Rose to determine, if possible, the views of the Emperor on these subjects. "And should the occasion seem favorable, inform yourself fully as to the probable terms and conditions upon which an agreement for mutual protection could be determined upon."[450]

The catastrophe that the General foresaw when he was writing the Mexican government in February 1865 finally overtook the Confederacy in April. However, by the time the news of Lee's surrender reached the headquarters of the Trans-Mississippi Department, Smith had changed his mind about leading his army into Mexico. When he addressed his army in Shreveport on April 21, he called on the soldiers of the Trans-Mississippi Army to stand by him on American soil and continue the fight.

"You possess the means of long resisting the invasion; you have hopes of succor from abroad," he said. "Protract the struggle and you will surely receive the aid of nations who already deeply sympathize with you.

"Stand by your colors, maintain your discipline. The great resources of this Department, its vast extent, the numbers, the discipline and efficiency of our army, will secure to our country terms that a proud people can with honor accept; and may, under the providence of God, be the means of checking the triumph of our enemy and securing the final success of our cause."[451]

Smith was preparing for the arrival of President Davis, who looked upon the region west of the Mississippi as "fair field" on which to make the final struggle of the war. An earlier effort had been made to cut Texas loose from the Confederacy and establish a "Lone Star Republic," to extend from the Gulf to the Pacific.[452]

The general feeling in the Department at that time was that not only could "Kirby-Smithdom," as it was called, offer resistance indefinitely, but that it could provide refuge for the defeated leaders of the Confederacy. At the North there was a similar feeling, and the newspapers[453] declared that the General had the means at hand to establish and maintain an empire.[454]

Smith called a public meeting at Shreveport on April 26 to consider deteriorating conditions, and the purport of all the speeches was continued resistance. Definite plans were laid to send a commissioner to meet the Confederate President and his cabinet, who Smith believed to be escaping to Havana, and to bring them by way of the Rio Grande to the Trans-Mississippi Department.[455]

18 CAPTAIN PARKER GOES TO GEORGIA

While General Edmund Kirby Smith was making plans to send a rescue party to Cuba to bring the President to the Trans-Mississippi Department, General Joseph Johnston was surrendering his troops in Durham, North Carolina, and President Davis was preparing to enter South Carolina.

Captain William Parker
Source: Library of Congress

And Captain Parker had again formed a wagon train in Abbeville, South Carolina, to set off across the country with the gold for Washington, Georgia.

"The news we got at different places along the route was bad," Parker said.[456]

"Unmerciful disaster followed fast and followed faster. We lightened ship as we went along—throwing away books, stationery and even as we heard the worst news, Confederate money. One could have traced us by these marks and formed an idea of the character of the news we were receiving."[457]

From Abbeville to Washington is about 50 miles, and Parker made the march in two days. "The first day after leaving Abbeville we crossed the Savannah River on a pontoon about 4 p.m. and went into camp for the night," he said. "We arrived at Washington the next day and here I heard that General Wilson USA had captured Macon (on April 20) with 10,000 cavalry and was on his way farther north so I resolved to halt for a time to deliberate."[458]

Parker had transferred the money to a nearby house and put a strong guard over it.[459] "The ladies were accommodated with rooms at the tavern," he said. "There were no meals served there but we had an abundance of provisions. Our coffee and sugar was as good as gold and by trading it for eggs, butter, poultry, and milk, we managed to keep up an excellent mess. All the men, teamsters and all, were allowed plenty of bacon, coffee and sugar, and if they were ragged, they were at all events fat and saucy."[460]

After a day's deliberation and consultation with some of the citizens of Washington, Parker decided to go to Augusta, Georgia. "I knew there was a general in command there and also a naval officer senior to myself and I thought I would at least have the benefit of their advice," he said. "We left the ladies behind at the tavern in Washington for we expected now a fight at any time. Affairs were looking very threatening."[461]

Parker left Washington on the cars for Augusta. "We were on a branch road and when we arrived at the junction with the main road across Georgia running from Augusta westward to Atlanta, we fell in with the train from Atlanta and stopped to allow it to pass.[462]

"Captain Rochelle went to inquire for news, and he soon returned with information that General Lee had surrendered on the 9th of April," Parker said. "To show how completely isolated we had been, it never entered my head that the news could be telegraphed via Nashville and

Atlanta. Our lines I knew were down and as I was the last to arrive from Danville, I supposed I had the latest news."[463] Parker thought that some speculator on his way to Augusta was circulating this news for his own purposes, and he directed Captain Rochelle to take a guard and arrest him.[464]

"Fortunately for him and for me too, I suppose, the man could not be found." Parker said. "We followed on after the mail train, and I really did not believe the report until it was confirmed to me upon our arrival at Augusta that night. We did not unpack the money from the cars in Augusta. The midshipmen bivouacked nearby. I called upon General Birkie Fry, who commanded the post, and upon Commodore William Hunter, senior naval officer present. There was a gunboat or two in the river which had escaped from Savannah."[465]

General Fry told Parker he could offer no hope of protection because he had but few troops and was expecting to surrender to General Wilson as soon as he appeared with his cavalry.[466]

"However, Generals Johnston and Sherman had just declared an armistice, and that gave us a breathing spell," Parker said. "The money remained in the cars, and the midshipmen and the Charlotte company lived in the depot. While in Augusta and afterwards, I was frequently advised by officious persons to divide the money among the Confederates, as the war was over, and it would otherwise fall into the hands of the Federal troops."[467]

The answer to this was that the war was not over as long as General Johnston held out, and that the money would be held intact until President Davis was met up with, Parker said.[468]

Johnston returned to Durham Station where he signed an agreement on April 18 with Sherman that provided generous terms of surrender for the Confederate government and included guaranteed rights of person and property and general amnesty for Confederates.[469] The agreement was far more generous than the terms under which Lee had surrendered on April 9.

While Johnston was negotiating with Sherman, Davis and the Confederate Cabinet and their military escort moved across North Carolina to arrive in Charlotte on April 19. The Confederates would be there seven days until April 26[470] with Davis staying in a house on East Trade Street (where the Charlotte Observer is located today).[471]

Sherman's pride and satisfaction in the surrender terms that marked the end of his herculean campaign through the swamps and rivers of Georgia and the Carolinas was short-lived. His proposed terms of surrender soon fell into a quagmire of political maneuvering in Washington, D.C., and Sherman was notified by Halleck and Stanton on April 23 that the agreement had been rejected. Even worse, the report on the rejection, which was published in the *New York Times* on April 24, implied that Sherman had opened a way for Jefferson Davis to escape to Mexico or Europe with his plunder when Sherman ordered Stoneman to withdraw from Salisbury, North Carolina.

The dispatch said: "It is stated here, by respectable parties, that the amount of specie taken south by Jeff. Davis and his partisans is very large, including not only the plunder of the Richmond banks, but previous accumulations. They hope, it is said, to make terms with General Sherman, or some other commander, by which they will be permitted, with their effects, including this gold plunder, to go to Mexico or Europe. Johnston's negotiations look to this end."[472]

Sherman was "outraged beyond measure." The bulletin from the Secretary of War "gave warrant to the impression, which was soon broadcast, that I might be bribed by banker's gold to permit Davis to escape," he said. "I regarded this bulletin of Mr. Stanton as a personal and official insult, which I afterward publicly resented."[473] Sherman had not realized that before his assassination, Lincoln had ordered Grant to proceed to Sherman's headquarters in North Carolina and direct operations against the enemy.[474]

Sherman said he had not known about the March 3 dispatch from Lincoln to Stanton that limited Grant and thus his subordinates to negotiations on purely military matters, even though at Savannah, Stanton had authorized Sherman to control all matters, civil and military. Stanton implied that Sherman had received a copy of the dispatch and had disobeyed orders. The newspaper article said that "General Sherman was ordered to resume hostilities immediately."[475]

Sherman was preparing to head back to Savannah by sea to meet officers stationed at Macon and Augusta when Stanton issued a second dispatch on April 27. The orders were for Generals Edward R. Canby and George Henry Thomas to disregard Sherman's arrangements with Johnston and to "push the enemy in every direction."[476]

The dispatch said that "Jeff. Davis's money was moving south from Goldsboro in wagons as fast as possible." Thomas and Wilson were warned not to obey any orders from Sherman and, along with Canby and all commanders on the Mississippi, were to take measures "to intercept the rebel chiefs and their plunder."[477] Sherman was outraged. "By this time, I was in possession of the second bulletin of Mr. Stanton, published in all the Northern newspapers, with

Generals Edward Canby (left) and George Thomas were ordered to disregard Sherman's surrender agreement and "push the enemy in every direction." Source: Library of Congress

comments that assumed that I was a common traitor and a public enemy; and high officials had even instructed my own subordinates to disobey my lawful orders," even though Sherman's command over North Carolina had never been revoked or modified.[478]

Stanton was insinuating that Sherman was allowing Davis to escape with wagon loads of "specie...estimated here at from six to thirteen million dollars."[479] Sherman was "shocked and insulted" by the tone of the dispatches coming out of Washington and the allegations that Davis had enough money to buy his escape from Sherman's army.[480]

Rumors were circulating about the vast amounts of gold and silver that had been hauled out of Richmond as the Confederate government collapsed. "The assertion that Jeff. Davis's specie-train, of six to thirteen million dollars, was reported to be moving south from Goldsboro in wagons as fast as possible, found plenty of willing ears, though my army of eighty thousand men had been at Goldsboro from March 22d to the date of his dispatch, April 26th and such a train would have been composed of from fifteen to thirty-two six-

Secretary of War Edwin Stanton *Source:*
Library of Congress

mule teams to have hauled this specie, even if it all were in gold."[481] Even though Sherman was still fuming over the allegations that he never denied, he sent word to Palmer, who was still in Dallas, North Carolina, that Lee's army had surrendered and that a general armistice had been declared. Assuming that the war was over, Palmer recalled Major John Herrick from Tuckasegee Ford and left for Knoxville. Palmer's brigade had gone as far as Hendersonville, North Carolina, on April 23, where they skirmished with a small force of Confederates and were met by a courier from Stoneman, who had reached Knoxville.[482]

"The dispatches brought by the courier contained the startling intelligence that President Lincoln had been assassinated, and the armistice suspended; also, an order directing Colonel Palmer to face about, and join, with all vigor and celerity, in the pursuit of President Davis, who, with his family, his personal staff, and what remained of his cabinet, was seeking to escape to the Gulf States."[483]

"In both brigades, officers and men were alike stunned and maddened by the wanton and cowardly murder of the President," Mason said. "It was with difficulty that Colonel Brown could restrain his Tennesseans from wreaking immediate vengeance upon Asheville.

"Yesterday, every soldier had rejoined in the armistice which marked, as they thought, the close of the war. Today, they sullenly rejoiced that the truce was broke, and that they could have another opportunity of avenging the foul crime at Washington. Carbines were reloaded, and at dawn, on the 27th of April, Palmer's brigade, again on a war footing, rode rapidly out of Hendersonville, in a southeasterly direction to begin the pursuit of Jefferson Davis."[484]

Stoneman's men had been so close to the Presidential entourage that their paths had crossed at Tuckasegee Ford on the Catawba River, which was one of the main reasons that Stanton and other government officials believed that Sherman had allowed Davis to escape through North Carolina when he could have been captured so easily.

Remembering Lincoln's wish that Davis and the other Confederate officials should escape, Sherman said in his memoirs that he didn't know at the time that the Johnson administration even wanted to capture the Confederate president. Lincoln's wishes for Davis and his other government officials to escape after the war were also well known to the members of Lincoln's cabinet and to General Grant.

In white-hot anger, Sherman wrote his old friend Grant on April 28. Sherman said he was furious that Stanton had taken his secret military communication with the cabinet to the newspapers, but even more outraged that he was being publicly accused of disobeying orders, insubordination and of taking a bribe to open an escape path for Davis by ordering Stoneman out of Salisbury.[485]

Still not denying that he had been bribed and quickly

shifting blame to Stoneman, Sherman said, "General Stoneman was not at 'Salisbury,' but had gone back to 'Statesville,'"(which was 26 miles west of Salisbury), Sherman said. "Davis was between us, and therefore Stoneman was beyond him. By turning toward me he was approaching Davis, and, had he joined me as ordered, I would have had a mounted force greatly needed for Davis's capture, and for other purposes. Even now I don't know that Mr. Stanton wants Davis caught, and as my official papers, deemed sacred, are hastily published to the world, it will be imprudent for me to state what has been done in that regard."[486]

Sherman lashed out at Stanton. "As the editor of the *Times* has logically and fairly drawn from this singular document the conclusion that I am insubordinate, I can only deny the intention."[487]

In his letter to Grant on April 28, Sherman said he had never in his life "questioned or disobeyed an order, though many and many a time I risked my life, health, and reputation, in obeying orders, or even hints to execute plans and purposes, not to my liking."[488]

Sherman described his four years in camp in which "I conferred freely with the best officers in this army as to the points involved in this controversy....They will learn with pain and amazement that I am deemed insubordinate, and wanting in commonsense; that I, who for four years have labored day and night, winter and summer, who have brought an army of seventy thousand men in magnificent condition across a country hitherto deemed impassable, and placed it just where it was wanted, on the day appointed, have brought discredit to our Government!

"I do not wish to boast of this, but I do say that it entitled me to the courtesy of being consulted before publishing to the world a proposition rightfully submitted to higher authority for adjudication, and then accompanied by statements which invited the dogs of the press to be let loose upon me."[489]

Sherman ended his letter to Grant on a bitter note. "I will therefore go on to execute your orders to the conclusion, and, when done, will with intense satisfaction leave to the civil authorities the execution of the task of which they seem so jealous."[490] And he demanded that his letter should be made public in the newspapers.

General U.S. Grant
Source: Library of Congress

19 CAPTAIN PARKER TRIES TO LEAVE THE GOLD

While Generals Johnston and Sherman were negotiating the surrender near Durham, North Carolina, Captain Parker reached Augusta, Georgia, and was trying to transfer responsibility but not control of the gold to Confederate officials.

He asked one of the Confederate Treasury Officers to take charge of the treasure and remain with it. "This he seemed disinclined to do," Parker said, so after consulting with the military, he agreed to continue guarding the treasure.[491]

Although he was anxious to be relieved of the moral responsibility of being the custodian of the money, he considered his command the best protectors and never asked to be relieved.[492] "I had no idea of giving up my control of it to any other command even if there had been one to assume it, which there was not.[493]

"The money had been confided to my keeping and I determined to hold it as long as the war lasted," Parker said. "The war was not over as some in Augusta would have had me to believe. So long as an army remained in the field the war to me existed. I knew that it must be soon over but what I mean to express is that until I knew that General Johnston, under whose command I now considered myself, had surrendered, my duty was plain to me."[494]

While in Augusta and afterwards Parker was approached by a number of soldiers and civilians who wanted to divide the money because they said that the war was over and it would otherwise fall into the hands of the Federal troops.[495]

"I was told that we would be attacked by our own men and might at the very end of the war fall by the hands of

The powder works factory in Augusta, Georgia, was still functioning at the end of the Civil War. The chimney is still visible today. *Source: Library of Congress*

our friends," Parker said. "To this I made but one reply. The treasure had been put in my keeping, and I would hold it until I met President Davis, and that, if necessary, the command would be killed in the defence (sic) of it. My officers and men stood firmly by me in this and all advances were met by a quiet reply to this effect."[496]

With an armistice between Johnston and Sherman in effect, Parker took up quarters at the hotel in Augusta[497] where he received a telegraphic dispatch from Secretary of the Navy Mallory directing him to disband his command.[498]

"Under the circumstances, I declined to do so," Parker said. "At this time we heard of the assassination of President Lincoln, an event which gave much pain to all with whom I conversed and which cast a gloom over all thinking men. It was universally condemned in the South but that goes without saying. On (April) 20th General Fry notified me that the armistice (between Johnston and Sherman) would end the next day and he advised me to move on."[499]

Secretary of the Navy Stephen Mallory ordered Captain Parker to disband his command.
Source: Library of Congress

Parker decided to turn back and try to meet President Davis in his retreat. "I knew he would cross the Savannah river at one of two points between Abbeville and Washington or lower down," Parker said. "After much reflection I determined to retrace my steps in the hope of intercepting him at some point on the former route. Accordingly we left Augusta on the 23d in the cars for Washington, Georgia again."[500]

When Parker decided to retrace his steps, he was thinking that President Davis would hear that Mrs. Davis had been left in Abbeville, where she was still staying with the Burts. News had been scarce in Abbeville, but a letter finally arrived from nearby Cokesbury Depot dated Saturday afternoon, 2:30 o'clock April 22, 1865:[501]

"Mrs. Davis. Madame: I have the honor, in compliance with my offer, to write from this place. I presume you heard the rumors of yesterday, viz., that an armistice of sixty days had been agreed upon, and General Grant had sent couriers to the different raiding parties to that effect; that commissioners to negotiate terms had been appointed, consisting on our part of Generals Lee, Johnston, and Beauregard, and on the part of the Yankees of Grant, Sherman."[502]

Weighed down with bad news, Mrs. Davis and her entourage set out the next day for Washington, Georgia. Meanwhile Parker left Augusta on April 23, arrived at Washington the same day, formed a train again, and started for Abbeville.[503]

20 JOHN WILKES BOOTH IS CAPTURED

While General Sherman was feuding with Secretary of War Stanton about the escaping Confederate president and the Confederate gold, Lincoln's assassins were making their way toward the Richard Henry Garrett Farm, which was located 60 miles south of Washington, D.C., near Port Royal, Virginia[504].[505]

"Booth made his escape from the rear of the theater immediately upon 9th Street, thence to Pennsylvania Avenue," according to Thomas A. Jones, a Maryland Confederate mail agent who would play the most significant role in the escape of the assassins. "When Booth reached the avenue, he rode toward the Capitol as far as 11th Street, then down 11th Street to the Navy Yard bridge (also known as the East Potomac Bridge) where he was joined by Herold, Jones said. They crossed the bridge unchallenged by the guards and took the road toward Surrattsville," a sparsely settled town located 10 miles away from Washington.[506]

Surrattsville, Maryland in 1865. Source: Library of Congress

After passing through swamps and timber so dense that they were almost lost, Booth and Herold reached the tavern in Surrattsville, Maryland, owned by John Lloyd and managed by Mary Surratt, where they picked up one of their carbines.[507]

Booth was too weak to carry the second carbine because he had fractured his leg when he caught his foot in the curtain at Ford's Theatre, according to Buckingham.[508] Booth's leg had become so painful that he abandoned his original intention of taking the shorter route to the river and crossing in the boat that had been placed at Port Tobacco, Maryland. Instead he took the road through Surrattsville, which was 10 miles away from Washington, and arrived in the early morning of April 15 at the home of Dr. Samuel A. Mudd, who lived three miles from Bryantown in the northeastern part of Charles County, Maryland, about 20 miles from Washington.[509]

"They contracted with him for twenty five dollars in greenbacks to set the broken leg," Townsend said.[510] Booth, who had met the doctor and visited at his house about 18 months before the assassination, told the doctor that his horse had fallen and hurt him. "How much they told Dr. Mudd beyond the fact that they wished to cross the river to Virginia, is not known," Jones said.[511]

While Herold was hunting for a carriage, Dr. Mudd rode out to visit patients and heard the news about Lincoln's assassination. By time Mudd returned home, Herold and Booth, who had been given a homemade crutch and shaved off his mustache,[512] mounted their horses and made their way to the home of the son of Jones' foster brother, Samuel Cox Jr., who hid them in the woods about a mile west of Jones' house.[513]

It was to this spot that Booth once told his fellow conspirators that they would bring President Lincoln to

be transported to Virginia, but it became the escape route for the assassins instead, Townsend said.

Jones was reluctant to help at first, but after meeting Booth, Jones enthusiastically promised to bring food and newspapers and help get them across the river, if possible.[514]

To keep from arousing suspicion, Herold led their horses that night into quick-sand in nearby Zekiah Swamp where they were shot and sank out of sight from their own weight, Jones said.[515]

"Whether my opinion is correct or not, it is certain that not even a bone of them has ever been discovered to this day."[516]

When Jones went to Port Tobacco the next day, he met Captain William Williams in the bar room of the old Brawner Hotel (which was later the St. Charles Hotel). Williams, who was a Washington (D.C.) City detective, was offering $100,000 to anyone who would provide information that would lead to Booth's capture.[517]

Jones, who had impressed the Federal officers and Union soldiers generally "as a man of rather slow wits, of an indolent mind with but little intelligence or interest in what was going on around him," returned to the fugitives near his farm without disclosing their whereabouts and claiming the reward.[518]

After Booth and Herold had hidden in the woods for six cool and foggy days, Jones said the cavalry had heard that Booth had been sighted in St. Mary's and the Federals galloped off in that direction.[519]

"'Now or never,' I thought, 'is my chance.'" Jones said.[520]

Booth, who Jones said was unable to stand, was raised onto Jones' horse, and with Jones in front showing the way and Herold leading the horse, they walked 3 ½

Garrett house where Booth died. *Source: Library of Congress*

miles in the darkness between 9 p.m. and 10 p.m. to Jones' farm and the river.[521] They waited at water's edge until Jones brought supper from his house for the two men and helped them into his boat. While Jones was pushing the boat into the Potomac River, Booth offered him money, and he accepted $18, "the price of the boat I knew I would never see again," he said.[522]

Jones never tried to reclaim his boat, which was recovered at the home of Mrs. Nicholas (Elizabeth) Quesenberry at Machadoc Creek in Virginia, where the assassins landed later that night. The mail route and Confederate signal station that connected to Jones' house in Maryland were located on her farm. The boat in which Booth crossed the Potomac was left with Mrs. Quesenberry, who helped them after they left Jones. The boat was quickly taken to Washington when she was arrested, but she was released almost immediately.[523]   The fugitives were taken in by Dr. Richard Stuart, the richest man in King George County, Virginia .[524] He had a large brick house at Mathias Point on the river and was entertaining guests when they arrived. He was annoyed to find that Lincoln's assassins were on his property now that the war was over, but sent them to an outbuilding, anyway. Booth and Herold left the next morning on their way to Port Conway on

Lieutenant Edward P. Doherty
Source: National Archives

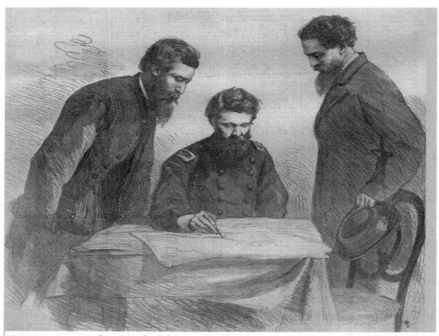

Lieutenant Doherty, (L-R) Colonel Baker and Colonel Conger plan the capture of John Wilkes Booth. *Source: Library of Congress*

The Federal cavalry set fire to the barn while Booth was still inside. *Source: Library of Congress*

the Rappahannock River. They crossed into Carolina County on April 24 to Richard H. Garrett's farm and found their last hiding place in his large barn.[525]

By then, Lieutenant Edward P. Doherty,[526] who was in command of the pursuing cavalry of 50 men, had discovered that the assassins were well-armed and hiding in Garrett's barn.[527] Specific orders were issued to the cavalry to take the fugitives alive.

Herold surrendered and was handcuffed to a tree, but in an effort to take Booth alive, the barn was set on fire. "As the roof of the barn was about falling in, and Booth looked like he was going to bolt, he was shot in the neck by Sergeant Boston Corbett of the Sixteenth New York, and died three hours later," Buckingham said.[528]

A soldier was dispatched for the nearest doctor, who was three miles away. Booth motioned for strong drink

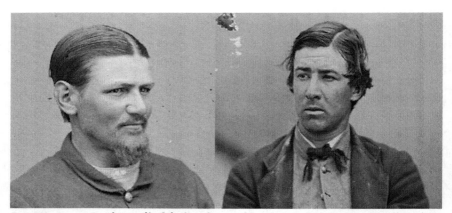

Sgt. Boston Corbett (left) disobeyed orders, shot into the flaming barn and killed Booth. David Herold (right) surrendered and left the barn before Booth was killed. *Source: Library of Congress*

every two minutes and made frequent desires to be turned over, not by speech but by gesture, and was alternately placed on his back, belly and side, Townsend said.

"Finally the fussy little doctor arrived in time to be useless," Townsend said. "He probed the wound to see if the ball were not in it and shook his head sagely and talked learnedly."[529]

After Booth died, "They sewed him up in a saddle blanket," Buckingham said. "This was his shroud too like a soldier's. They found about him bills of exchange, Canada money and a diary....Booth's only arms were his carbine, knife and two revolvers."[530]

Herold was released for the march, and Colonel Conger immediately pushed on for Washington. The cortege was to follow. As the soldiers searched for a way to take Booth's body back to Washington, they found a man living in the vicinity who "had the misfortune to possess a horse," Townsend said. "This horse was a relic of former generations and showed by his protruding ribs the general leanness of

Ruins of Garrett's barn. *Source: Library of Congress*

the land. He moved in an eccentric amble and when put upon his speed was generally run backward."[531]

To this horse was harnessed "a very shaky and absurd wagon which rattled like approaching dissolution and each part of it ran without any connection or correspondence with any other part. It had no tailboard and its shafts were sharp as famine and into this mimicry of a vehicle the murderer was to be sent to the Potomac river[532] to the Navy Yard at Washington."[533]

During an autopsy, three of Booth's cervical vertebrae were removed and became part of the collection of the National Museum of Health and Medicine in Washington, D.C., but witnesses gave different accounts of what happened to Booth's body.

Colonel William P. Wood with the U.S. Secret Service said, "The body of Booth was taken off the steam (John S.) Ide, April 27th, 1865, down the Potomac River; from the steam it was placed on a boat by Capt. Baker and his nephew, a lieutenant in the New York Seventy-First Volunteers, and carried to an island twenty-seven miles from Washington (D.C), and secretly buried there."[534]

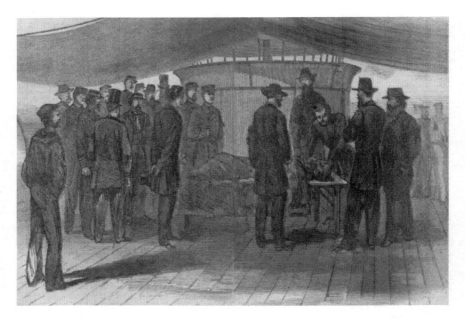

Autopsy of Booth's body on board the monitor Montauk.
Source: Library of Congress

In 1893, Captain W. E. Hillard, of Metropolis, Illinois, said: "I was one of four privates who carried the remains of Booth from the old Capital Prison in Washington to a gunboat, which carried them about ten miles down the Potomac river, when the body was sunk in the river, etc."[535]

General Lew Wallace said on January 27, 1898, that Booth was buried under a brick pavement in a room of the old prison of Washington City, and was later transferred to Baltimore at the request of his friends.[536][537]

Although Buckingham and Jones had no first-hand knowledge of the burial, they both said in later years that they believed that Booth was buried under the prison floor in the Washington Arsenal grounds in what became Ft. Leslie J. McNair.[538]

"About four years afterward, when the prison was abolished and the walls pulled down," Jones said,[539] the body was exhumed and delivered to Booth's brother Edwin who had him interred in an unmarked grave in the family lot in Green Mount Cemetery in Baltimore.[540]

Controversy erupted 28 years later over whether the body that was buried in the Arsenal grounds had actually been Booth.

The suicide of David E. George in Enid, Oklahoma, on January 14, 1893, and his deathbed confession raised questions about whether Booth had even died in Garrett's barn. Instead, George, who was also known under the alias of John St. Helen by his lawyer Finis L. Bates, claimed that he was Booth and that a plantation worker named "Ruddy," who was carrying his personal effects, had been mistakenly killed in his place in the Garrett barn. All of George's physical attributes were identical to Booth, according to numerous witnesses including General D.D. Dana, of Lubec, Maine, who identified the body on January 17, 1903, Bates said. The mummified remains of George, which were displayed around the country, were also identified as Booth by his oldest living nephew Junius Brutus Booth III of Boston, Massachusetts, on February 21, 1903, at Memphis, Tennessee, according to Bates.[541]

And George's body was identified as Booth by actor Joe Jefferson, "the world's famous Rip Van Winkle," at Memphis, Tennessee, on April 14, 1903, Bates said. Jefferson had made appearances on stage with Booth for several years, Bates said.[542] Before his suicide, the man who had been known as both George and John St. Helen had provided such a detailed account of the assassination that Bates believed his story,[543] as did thousands of others who came to view his body.[544]

As St. Helen told Bates that Vice President Johnson was part of the conspiracy. Quoting St. Helen, Bates said that Booth and Herold, with others, had tried for a year

David E. George, a 64-year-old man who committed suicide January 13, 1903, in Enid, Oklahoma, persuaded his lawyer before he died that he was John Wilkes Booth. His swollen and mummified body shown here 11 days after his death was identified by several who had known him as Booth, and the body was displayed around the country. The Escape and Suicide of John Wilkes Booth by Finis L. Bates, Applewood, Carlisle, Mass., 1907)

and a half to kidnap Lincoln to take him to Richmond as a hostage of war. "We came to Washington that day (April 14) to make a final successful effort, but when we arrived in the city, we learned that General Lee had surrendered," St. Helen said. "We went immediately to the Kirkwood Hotel to meet Vice President Andrew Johnson, and told him further efforts to kidnap the President were now useless, when Johnson remarked: 'Will you falter at this supreme moment?' When Booth could not understand his meaning, Johnson said: 'Are you too faint-hearted to kill him?'"[545]

Booth had said he would not attempt the assassin-nation because

General and Mrs. Grant were to be in the President's box at Ford's Theater that night, according to St. Helen. But Johnson agreed to arrange for the Grants to be elsewhere that night and gave Booth the password 'T.B' or 'T.B. Road' to cross unchallenged over the bridge afterwards, St. Helen said.[546]

"Johnson told Booth that since he would become president, that he could 'depend on him for protection and absolute pardon, if need be," St. Helen said."[547] Booth thought Johnson would be kinder to the south and would protect the people of the former Confederacy from oppression and confiscation of their remaining property. "By the killing of President Lincoln, I could practically bring victory to the Southern people out of defeat for the South, " St. Helen said.[548]

With the discovery of DNA testing, the controversy re-emerged at the end of the 20th century and is still alive. Family members trying to solve the mystery were denied permission to exhume the body purported to be Booth in 1995 when a judge ruled that its location in the cemetery could not be conclusively determined. The family members renewed their efforts in April 2013 by asking for DNA testing on the three cervical vertebra that had been removed during the autopsy in 1865. Descendants want to compare DNA with Booth's brother Edwin. Even though the family enlisted assistance from Congress, their request was denied, but the family has not given up.[549]

Herold was imprisoned in the Arsenal until he and other members who were believed to be part of the conspiracy, including Payne, Atzerodt, Mrs. Surratt, Dr. Mudd, and Spangler, were tried by a military commission.[550]

Jones and Cox were arrested a few days after the man believed to be Booth was killed, and they were kept prisoner in the old brick tavern at Bryantown in southern Maryland, the same tavern where Booth had stopped 18 months earlier while plotting to kidnap Lincoln.[551] A week later they were moved to the old Carroll prison in Washington.[552]

John T. Ford, the manager of the theater in which Lincoln was killed; Junius Brutus Booth, who was John Wilkes Booth's brother; John S. Clark, a comedian who was Booth's brother-in-law; and Dr. Richard Stuart were all in prison with Jones charged with complicity in the assassination. Other prisoners with them but not charged in the conspiracy included Governors Henry A. Wise of Virginia, Zebulon Vance of North Carolina, Joseph E. Brown of Georgia, and Barnes Compton of Maryland.[553]

After Jones was arrested, detectives sat in the street under his prison window describing how he was to be hanged. Jones continued urging Cox to admit nothing, and Jones was released after six weeks and Cox after seven weeks.[554]

After the war, Jones, who was a widower and the father of eight children, remarried and added two more children to his family. Although he had played the most significant role in Booth's escape, he was never charged in the conspiracy and never brought to trial, and he watched while others who had played much smaller roles were sentenced to jail terms or hanged. He kept his secret for 28 years while he worked for the government in Maryland and Baltimore and in a coal, wood and feed yard in north Baltimore.[555]

He finally broke his silence near the end of his life in 1893 when he wrote a 126-page book describing the role he had played in the conspiracy. He died two years later in 1895 at the age of 74 and is buried in Saint Mary's Catholic Cemetery in Newport, Charleston County, Maryland.[556]

Garrett, whose barn was the last hiding place for Booth and Herold, was never arrested or charged in the conspiracy.

21 THE FATE OF THE RICHMOND GOLD

Just as President Davis had predicted, the Johnson administration rejected the terms agreed to by General Johnston and General Sherman on April 24. "Whatever hope others entertained that the war was about to be peacefully ended, was soon dispelled by the rejection of the basis of the agreement by the Government of the United States, and a notice from Sherman of the termination of the armistice in forty-eight hours after noon of April 24th," Davis said. A vindictive policy had been speedily substituted for Lincoln's, "which avowedly was to procure a surrender of our forces in the field upon any terms, to stop the further effusion of blood."[557]

Still in Durham, Johnston met again with Sherman

Scene at Bennett House near Durham, N.C., where Johnston surrendered to Sherman. *Harper's Weekly, May 27, 1865.* Source: Ernest F. Hollings Special Collections Library, University of South Carolina.

who supplied new surrender conditions from the Johnson Administration. And even though Johnston had received specific orders sent by President Davis from Charlotte,[558] Johnston ignored the explicit orders, accepted the new terms and surrendered on April 26.[559]

Johnston disobeyed orders from President Davis and surrendered to Sherman on April 26. *Harper's Weekly, May 27, 1865.* Source: Ernest F. Hollings Special Collections Library, University of South Carolina.

While Johnston was disobeying orders and surrendering to Sherman, President Davis, who was still intent on reaching the Trans-Mississippi Department, was riding out of Charlotte in broad daylight, attended by all but two members of his cabinet, his personal staff, and a cavalry of about 2,000 soldiers from five brigades.

Though reduced in number, Davis said they were "in a good state of efficiency, and among their officers were some of the best in our service."[560]

Davis would say later that Johnston, by disobeying his orders and surrendering his army, had put everything at the mercy of the conquerors, "without making a movement to secure terms that might have availed to protect the political rights of the people and preserve their property from pillage when it was in his power."

Davis felt that an attempt by Johnston to make it to

the Trans-Mississippi Department might have turned out to be Johnston's most valuable service to the people of the South and "should have tempered the violence of Sherman's assaults upon some others who were exerting themselves in behalf of the South."[561]

Johnston's troops were paroled, and the officers were permitted to retain their side arms, baggage, and private

General Wade Hampton
Source: Library of Congress

horses. The total number of prisoners paroled at Greensboro, as reported by General John Schofield, was 36,817; in Georgia and Florida, as reported by General James H. Wilson, 52,543; in all under General Johnston, 89,360.[562]

Davis had concurred when General Lee had surrendered to overwhelming force and insurmountable difficulties,[563] but he would never forgive Johnston for surrendering without some favorable terms for the South. Davis had visualized numerous advantages for the Confederacy if Johnston had retreated to the west.

"The surrender of Johnston was a different affair," Davis said. "Johnston's line of retreat, as chosen by himself through South Carolina, was open and had supplies placed upon it at various points. He had a large force, of which over 36,000 were paroled at Greensborough, N. C.

"We had other forces in the field, and we were certainly in a position to make serious resistance. This was all the more important, as such ability would have been of service in securing better terms in bringing the war to an end."[564]

Sherman and Grant were both eager for Johnston to surrender at Durham because both correctly feared that Davis could have continued the war in the Trans-Mississippi Department where General Smith had access to 60,000 soldiers and was negotiating for support with Mexico, which was sympathetic to the Confederacy.

Grant wrote, "For my own part, I think that Johnston's tactics were right. Anything that could have prolonged the war a year beyond the time that it finally did close, would probably have exhausted the North to such an extent that they might then have abandoned the contest and agreed to a settlement."[565]

General Wade Hampton also wanted to continue withdrawing to the region across the Mississippi, which had been Davis' objective all along.

However, Lee, who was in Richmond by then, wrote, "I believe an army cannot be organized or supported in Virginia" or for that matter east of the Mississippi. He said he was opposed to a partisan war and recommended suspension of hostilities and restoration of peace.[566]

The President spent the night in the Bratton home in York, S.C., on April 27. *Photo by Pat McNeely*

Intent on reaching the Trans-Mississippi Department, the Confederate president and his escort slipped quietly over the Catawba River at Nation's Ford into South Carolina on April 26 and headed for Fort Mill in York County. The exact site where he crossed the river is apparently not known today, but it is believed to have at been at Nation's Ford near the railroad bridge that Palmer's men burned before skirting Charlotte on their way to Hendersonville. As the Davis entourage crossed the Catawba into South Carolina, Palmer's brigade was camped in Dallas, 25 miles west of Charlotte.

Unaware that Stoneman's men had been close enough to capture him several times in the past few weeks and of the accusations being leveled at Sherman by the Johnson administration about his escape through

President Davis had lunch in the home of General William Henry Wallace as he passed through Union, S.C., on April 28. *Photo by Pat McNeely*

North Carolina, Davis and his cabinet spent the night of April 26 about 15 miles south of Charlotte near Fort Mill, South Carolina. They were guests at the homes of Colonel Andrew Baxter Springs and Colonel William Elliott White. Davis held another cabinet meeting on the lawn of White's house, where he accepted Trenholm's resignation as secretary of the treasury. Trenholm, who was ill, had reached his home state of South Carolina and had decided that he could no longer perform his duties.[567] Postmaster General John H. Reagan was appointed as his successor at Fort Mill.[568]

Davis spent the night of April 27 in the home of Dr. James Rufus Bratton at 8 Congress Street, York, in York County and continued on his journey toward Abbeville on April 29.[569]

Detail of the entrance to the home of General William Henry Wallace in Union, S.C. Photo by Pat McNeely

Davis' path of retreat took him through Union County, South Carolina, on April 28 and 29, where he made several stops including dining at the noon meal at General William Henry Wallace's house in the 400 block of East Main Street in Union.[570]

Davis' evening meal that day was at the home of Civil War casualty J.R.R. Giles, one mile south of Rose Hill, where they spent the night and had breakfast on April 30. That house doesn't exist today. Their last stop in Union County was for the noon meal at the Cross Keys House before continuing their journey through Laurens County on their way to Abbeville.

As Davis made his way through South Carolina, Sherman was watching the rising turmoil and confusion in Washington. He "then realized the national loss in the death at that critical moment of Mr. Lincoln, who had long pondered over the difficult questions involved, who, at all events, would have been honest and frank, and would not have withheld from his army commanders at least a hint that would have been to them a guide. It was plain to me, therefore, that the manner of his assassination had stampeded the civil authorities in Washington, had unnerved them, and that that they were then undecided as to the measures indispensably necessary to prevent anarchy at the South."[571]

As the war stumbled to an end, Sherman was beginning to believe that President Johnson was bitter and vindictive in his feelings toward the South, and he could see the "wild pressure of every class of politicians to enforce on their new President their pet schemes."[572]

Sherman summoned his army and corps commanders together on April 28 at his headquarters at the governor's mansion in Raleigh where he explained what had happened and distributed orders for the future. Generals John Schofield, Alfred Terry and Judson Kilpatrick were to remain on duty in the Department of North Carolina, already commanded by Schofield, and the right and left wings were to march north by easy stages to Richmond, where they would wait for him to return from the south.

As Sherman was gathering his troops in Raleigh on April 30, the Confederate President was leaving Cross Keys, South Carolina, in Union County accompanied by his cabinet and his military escort made up of elements of five brigades. Mrs. Mary Whitmire Davis, who owned the Cross Keys House at that time, afterwards told her descendants the story of President Davis' luncheon at the house.[573] Reenactments of Davis' visit are still held annually at Cross Keys.

They arrived at Riser's Brick House (on S.C. 66, 7 miles northeast of Joanna and known then as Martin's Depot) in the afternoon of April 30 and passed through Martin's Depot (the name was later changed to Joanna), South Carolina.[574]

Davis spent the night of April 30 with his cabinet and other high- ranking officers at the home of Lafayette Young, 2.5 miles southwest of Joanna in Laurens County. Davis, who had arrived there from Union, left early the next morning for Cokesbury and Abbeville.[575] Davis spent the night of May 1 in the home of the mother of General

Annual reenactments are held at Cross Keys house in Union, S.C.
Photo by Pat McNeely

Martin Witherspoon Gary, son of Dr. Thomas Reeder Gary and Mary Ann Porter) in Cokesbury (which was in Abbeville District then, but is now in Greenwood County). The house is the Old Cokesbury and Masonic Female College and Conference School in Greenwood County and was the site of another cabinet meeting.[576] As Davis was crossing through South Carolina toward Abbeville, Parker was heading back from Washington, Georgia, toward the same destination.

"On the way we met Mrs. President Davis and family escorted by Mr. Burton Harrison the President's private secretary," Parker said. "They could give me no news as to the whereabouts of the President. I have forgotten where they told me they intended to go. They had a comfortable ambulance and two very fine led horses which I thought they would very likely lose."[577]

By then, Parker was tired of guarding the treasure. "In crossing the Savannah river I remember saying to Captain Rochelle that if the money were mine, I would throw it overboard rather than be longer burdened with it," Parker said. "I had had it nearly thirty days. The midshipmen were suffering for shoes, hats and clothing, and the care and responsibility weighed upon me."[578]

Parker had returned to Abbeville on April 28 and stored the treasure in a warehouse on the public square and placed a guard over it. "As before I also kept a strong patrol in the town which was now full of General Lee's paroled soldiers on their way to their homes," Parker said. "Threats were frequently made by these men to seize the money but they always received the same reply."[579]

Abbeville was on the direct route south and all the Trans-Mississippi troops passed through it as well as others. "The citizens had known but little of the sufferings of war," Parker said. "They were very kind and hospitable to us."[580]

On the night of the May 1, Parker was invited to a May party, which he attended more to find out what was going on in the town than anything else.[581]

While there, a paroled officer of General Samuel McGowan's brigade approached him and said he had information that the paroled men intended to attack the treasure that night and he thought it his duty to tell me. [582]

"I thanked him and went to my quarters where I issued orders to double the guard and patrol," Parker said. " I had given directions as soon as I arrived in Abbeville that a train and engine should be held ready for me with steam up at all hours of the day and night. My intention was, if threatened by the enemy, to run by steam to Newberry and then take to the dirt road again."[583]

Everything seemed quiet so Parker went to bed about

midnight leaving directions with the officer of the guard to call him if anything occurred. He had quarters in a private house and was sleeping on the floor of the parlor so he could be easily aroused.[584]

About 3 o'clock in the morning, the officer of the guard tapped at his window. "I can hear him now: 'Captain,' said he in a low voice, 'the Yankees are coming,'" Parker said. "Upon inquiry, I learned that a detachment of Federal cavalry had captured two gentlemen at Anderson (South Carolina) about thirty miles distant the evening before. One of the gentlemen had escaped and brought the news to Abbeville and, as Mr. Peek told me, thought the Federals would arrive about daylight. I immediately called all hands and packed the money in the cars and by daybreak had everybody on the train in readiness to move."[585]

Jefferson Davis signing government papers along the road.
Illustrated London News, July 22, 1865. *Source: Ernest F. Hollings Special Collections Library, University of South Carolina*

Parker stayed on the platform of the train to Newberry because he had not quite decided to run. "About sunrise we saw a company of cavalry winding down the hills in the distance, and I sent out two scouts who shortly returned with the information that it was the advance guard of President Davis' escort," Parker said. "So I had judged rightly in returning to Abbeville."[586]

President Davis and his Cabinet rode into town about 10 a.m. on May 2 and "were well received by the population of Abbeville," Parker said. "It was a sad enough sight to me. I know it reminded me of scenes I had witnessed in Central American revolutions. President Davis and his Cabinet (save Messrs. Trenholm and (Attorney General George) Davis) rode in." They were escorted by four skeleton brigades of cavalry—not more than 1,000 badly armed men in all. Parker thought these brigades belong to Generals Basil W. Dukes, George Gibbes Dibrell, John C. Vaughan and Samuel W. Ferguson. "The train was a long one. There were many brigadier-generals present — General Braxton Bragg among them—and wagons innumerable," Parker said.[587]

At Abbeville, the Treasury officers reported the train at the depot, having been a part of the time under the escort of Admiral Raphael Semmes's little naval force to protect it from the Federal cavalry, who were raiding on a parallel line with their route between them and the mountains.

On the evening of May 2, Parker and the guards turned the Confederate treasury over to the acting Secretary of the Treasury and was instructed to deliver it to the care of General Basil Duke, which he did at the railroad station.[588] Since Trenholm, the Secretary of the Treasury, had been left quite ill near the Catawba River (near Fort Mill), Postmaster and acting Secretary of the

Treasury Reagan "placed the coin under charge of the cavalry to convoy it (back) to Washington, Ga."[589]

"I had several interviews with President Davis and found him calm and composed, and resolute to a degree," Parker said. "As soon as I saw Mr. Mallory he directed me to deliver the treasure to General Basil Duke and disband my command. I went to the depot, and there, in the presences of my command, transferred it accordingly. General Duke was on horseback, and no papers passed."[590]

The Charlotte company immediately started for home. "I have a dim recollection that a keg of cents was presented to Captain (W. Kemp) Tabb for distribution among his men and that the magnificent present was indignantly declined," Parker said.[591]

"The treasure was delivered to General Duke *intact* so far as I knew," although he said some of it had been taken at Danville *by authority*.[592] The treasure on Parker's train had been guarded by the Confederate midshipmen for thirty days and preserved by them. "In my opinion this is what no other organization could have done in those days," Parker said.[593]

Davis spent the night of May 2 at the home of Colonel Armistead Burt, where he met with Breckenridge, the last Secretary of War, and Generals Bragg, Dibrill, Duke, Vaughn and Ferguson.

Davis was adamant in his convictions that the war should be continued. He explained his plan to go to the Trans-Mississippi region and build a new army, using the depleted cavalry units as a nucleus.

"When the brigade commanders were asked for their opinion, all of them expressed the opinion that they felt a prolongation of the fighting would only result in a needless waste of Southern lives and that the time had come to lay down their arms.[594] "By Mr. Mallory's order I then immediately disbanded my command and the Charlotte company marched off for home before I left the depot," Parker said.

"It was difficult to acknowledge that the Confederacy was broken. Some of them were throwing away or selling their arms as they looked upon the war as over.[595] There were many noble spirits among them who were ready and anxious to follow and defend the President to the death but the force taken as an organization was demoralized."[596]

The President went to Burt's house, and Parker, after finishing his duties involved with transferring the treasure and disbanding his command, called on Davis. "I never saw the President appear to better advantage than during these last hours of the Confederacy."[597]

"His personal appearance has been often described. I remember him as a slender man of about 5 feet 10 inches in height and with a grey eye as his most marked feature. His deportment was singularly quiet and dignified. At this time he showed no signs of despondency. His air was resolute, and he looked as he is, a born leader of men. His cabinet officers with the exception of General Breckenridge and Mr. Reagan stood, I thought, rather in awe of him. General Breckenridge presented his usual bold cavalier manner, but Secretary of the Navy Mallory and Secretary of State Benjamin were much depressed and showed it. I do not recall Mr. Reagan. He was the Postmaster General and acting Secretary of the Treasury. Mr. Trenholm, Secretary of the Treasury, and Mr. George Davis, Attorney General, had been taken ill by the way and were not with the party."[598]

"In addition to the four brigades of cavalry the President had in company more Brigadier Generals than I thought were in the army," Parker said. "Many of them had ambulances and wagons and the train must have been several miles long. It seemed to me that it was half a day coming in. Referring to the Federal cavalry I have alluded to, it was said that it was marching on Abbeville when it met Mr. Davis' escort and turned back. I never knew the truth of this report."[599]

After shaking hands with President Davis whom Parker found alone, he first gave him an account of taking the Davis family from Charlotte and told him of having met his wife a few days before on his way back to Abbeville. "He thanked me and then inquired after my command," Parker said. "I told him I had disbanded it. He said 'Captain, I am very sorry to hear that' and repeated it several times. I told him I had but obeyed Mr. Mallory's order, that my command had been on the march for thirty days and was without shoes and proper clothing."[600]

"The President seemed to be in deep thought for a few moments and I, wishing him clearly to appreciate my position, said, 'Mr. President, I must beg you to understand that I acted upon the peremptory order of the Secretary of the Navy.' He then replied, 'Captain, I have no fault to find with you, but I am very sorry Mr. Mallory gave you the order.' After seeing the escort, I understood Mr. Davis' regret."[601]

Parker told the President about his trip to Augusta and of General Wilson's movements and asked him what he proposed to do. He told Parker he would remain four days in Abbeville. "I then mentioned the affair of the previous night and said I looked upon his capture as inevitable if he prolonged his stay," Parker said. "He replied that he would never desert the Southern people, that he had been elected by them to the office he held and would stand by them. He gave me to understand that he

President Davis crossing the Georgia ridge five days before his capture. Source: Library of Congress

would not take any step which might be construed into an inglorious flight. He was most impressive on this point."[602]

The mere idea that he might be looked upon as fleeing seemed to arouse him, Parker said. "He got up and paced the floor and repeated several times that he would never abandon his people. I stuck to my text and said, 'Mr. President, if you remain here, you will be captured. You have about you only a few demoralized soldiers and a train of camp followers three miles long. You will be captured and you know how we will all feel about that. It is your duty to the Southern people not to allow yourself to be made a prisoner. Leave now with a few followers and cross the Mississippi, as you express a desire to do eventually, and there again raise the standard."[603]

The interview lasted an hour and Parker used every argument he could think of to induce the President to leave Abbeville, but it was in vain, Parker said. "He insisted that he would remain four days."[604]

After leaving the President Parker found Mallory and Benjamin waiting for him, with Benjamin very nervous and impatient to continue the retreat. "Mr. Mallory was more phlegmatic but was of my opinion that they would all be captured if they remained," Parker said.[605]

During the afternoon the soldiers packed the treasure in the wagons again preparatory to moving. "After it was taken away from Abbeville, which was on that night, I have no further personal knowledge of it," Parker said. "The admirable letter of Captain M.H. Clark published in the Southern Historical Society papers December 1881 gives the best account of it I have seen."[606]

Parker asked Mr. Mallory to come to his quarters to tea that evening, and at about 8 o'clock, Benjamin came in. "He begged me to see the President again and to urge him to leave," Parker said. "After some demur I consented to do so. I found Mr. Davis alone as before and apologizing for my intrusion said my intense anxiety for his safety must excuse it. I remained some time and saw that he had a better appreciation of the condition of affairs in Georgia than when I had seen him in the morning."[607]

All agreed the only hope was for Davis to elude nearby U.S. cavalry and escape west.[608] "I proposed to him that he should leave Abbeville with four naval officers of whom I was to be one and escape to the east coast of Florida," Parker said. "The object of taking naval officers was that they might seize a vessel of some kind and get to Cuba or the Bahamas, but this he rejected."[609]

After Parker left the President at 9 o'clock, Davis sent one of his aides to call the Cabinet together. "I went to my quarters and not long after received a note from Mr. Mallory saying they would leave that night, and he notified me so that I might accompany them if I desired," Parker said. "As they were all mounted, and I was on foot and could not get a horse, I was obliged to decline."[610]

The President and the cabinet decided that the command would be broken up, allowing the troops to choose for themselves if they wished to accept the terms of Johnston's surrender or to continue in their westward retreat. [611]

Unknown to Davis and his escort as they were leaving Abbeville on May 2, President Johnson issued Proclamation 131 providing a $100,000 reward for the arrest of the Confederate President. The proclamation said that evidence from the Bureau of Military Justice in the murder of Lincoln and the attempted assassination of Seward were "incited, concerted, and procured" by Davis. The proclamation also included $25,000 rewards for the arrest of Clement C. Clay, Jacob Thompson of Mississippi, George N. Sanders, Beverley Tucker, as well as a $10,000 reward for the arrest of William C. Cleary, who had been Clay's clerk.[612] All except Davis had been secret agents in Canada and at least one might have been visited by Booth in late 1864, according to Townsend.[613]

Northern newspaper editors who had been calling for treason charges against Davis quickly expanded their agenda to include conspiracy in the assassination of Lincoln. [614][615]

Unaware of the presidential proclamation and the price on his head, Davis and his escort left the Burt-Stark House in Abbeville for Washington, Georgia,[616] and crossed the Savannah River early on the morning of May 3.[617] "(We) rode some miles to a farmhouse, where I halted to get breakfast and have our horses fed," Davis said. "Here I learned that a regiment of the enemy was moving upon Washington, Ga., which was one of our depots of supplies, and I sent back a courier with a pencil-note addressed to General (John C.) Vaughan, or the officer commanding the advance, requesting him to come on and join me immediately."[618]

The house where the Confederates stopped was the first house they came to in Lincoln County, Georgia, after crossing the pontoon bridge across the Savannah River, and, according to Mary House Lane, who wrote about the incident in 1925, was the home of her sister, Mrs. David Moss.[619]

Davis and his escort stayed only long enough to water their horses and eat breakfast. Secretary of War Breckinridge, who was trailing behind, caught up with the cavalry and train that night while they were still halted at the Moss house.[620]

Stopping, Breckinridge learned from the officers that the men were "dissatisfied at the position of affairs; that they were guarding a train that could not be carried safely much farther; the Federal cavalry were known to be in full force not a great distance off; the destination and disposition of their own force was an uncertain one; their paper money was worthless for their needs; that they might never reach Washington, Georgia, with it, etc."[621]

A crowd gathered around when Breckinridge made a little speech, appealing to their honor as Confederate soldiers not to violate the trust reposed in them, but to remain Southern soldiers and gentlemen; and that when they reached Washington with the train, fair payments should be made.[622] "The men responded frankly, saying they proposed to violate no trust; they would guard it, but expressed what they considered due to them in the matter," Parker said, "and, as they would be paid some money in Washington, Ga., and no one could tell what would happen before they reached Washington, there was no good reason for delay."[623]

Breckinridge said that if they wished instant compliance with his promise, he would redeem it at once and ordered up the train to the house where he had stopped and the contents of seven wagons unloaded in the Mosses' living room;[624] the quartermasters were ordered to make out their pay-rolls after a certain amount was counted out and turned over to the proper officers.[625]

The troops were to be paid $108,322.90 to be divided among the members of the escort at the Moss house out of treasury funds. Meanwhile, a guard composed of five members of each brigade was posted over the treasure.[626]

Lane said the Confederates unloaded the contents of seven wagons in her sister's living room.[627] "The paymaster paid off the...commanders out the living room window," Lane wrote.[628] The troops were instructed to line up and hold out their hats, and each man was paid off with a five- dollar gold piece and $21.25 in silver.

Although Parker's command did not leave Abbeville with the Davis escort, Parker had yielded to the solicitations of his officers and had sent Paymaster John F. Wheliss[629] after them to see if he could secure enough money from Reagan to enable them to get back to their homes.

When they returned, "The boys told me they got about twenty-six dollars apiece; enough, they hoped, to take them through," Parker said.[630]After the pay-out at the Moss house, the wagons were reloaded and headed toward Washington, carrying with them the remainder of the treasure that Parker had guarded since the night of April 2 in Richmond. Benjamin and the treasure wagons camped near Washington on May 4. During the night after

Davis arrived in Washington, Breckinridge sent in an application for authority to draw from the treasury, under the protection of the troops, enough to make to them a partial payment.

Next morning, Colonel William Preston Johnston told Davis that Reagan, who was interim treasurer, had applied for M.H. Clark to act as Treasurer to take charge of the Treasury matters, and Clark was appointed acting Treasurer on May 4. "I authorized the acting Secretary of the Treasury to meet the requisition by the use of the silver coin in the train," Davis said.[631]

And it was on May 4 in Washington, Georgia, that the Richmond bank train was separated from the treasury train. Parker said the funds were never mixed. And Secretary of the Treasury Reagan said that no handling or accounting of the money was necessary but merely permission for the cashiers and tellers to take control of their own matters." The bank officials transferred their specie to the vault of the old branch bank of the State of Georgia, which was in the house that was occupied by Doctor J. J. Robertson, the cashier of the branch bank. It was in the Robertson building that Davis signed his last official document of the Confederate States of America.[632] It was the last official signature President Davis affixed to any paper of the Confederacy.[633]

The $450,000 from the Richmond banks would remain in the Robertson bank vault in Washington, until May 24, when—fourteen days after Davis was captured—the bank funds would be loaded into five wagons and covered with canvas to look like apple vendors to begin the return trip to Abbeville, South Carolina.[634]

Acting Secretary of the Treasury Clark rode out to General Basil Duke's camp on May 4 where the remaining government specie from Richmond was turned over to him. Although Parker said the Confederate treasury contained $500,000 when he left Richmond, Clark said the treasury contained only $327,022.90 in gold and silver bullion when it left Danville. Out of that, officers paid $39,000 to soldiers in Greensboro, but no one ever accounted for $172,977.10 that seemed to have disappeared between Richmond and Danville.

Clark sat down under the shade of a large elm tree, which he had established as the Confederate Treasury Department. With permission from Breckinridge and Reagan, Clark's first act was to burn enormous amounts of Confederate money.[635]

"I obtained permission from General Breckinridge and Mr. Reagan to burn a mass of currency and bonds, and burnt millions in their presence," he said.[636]

While Clark was settling up some treasury accounts, Davis told Captain Given Campbell, of Kentucky, that his company was not strong enough to fight and too large to pass without observation. Davis asked Campbell to inquire if there were ten men who would volunteer to go with him without question wherever he should choose. "He brought back for answer that the whole company volunteered on the terms proposed," Davis said. "I was gratified, but felt to accept the offer would expose them to unnecessary hazard, and told him, in any manner he might think best, to form a party of ten men."[637]

Clark's last payment outside of Washington, Ga., was "of eighty-six thousand dollars ($86,000) in gold coin and gold bullion, to a trusted officer of the Navy, taking his receipt for its transmission out of the Confederacy, to be held for the Treasury Department...before Judge Reagan and myself left Washington, Ga.[638] The trusted officer was Mallory's paymaster, who concealed the money in a false bottom of a carriage and attempted to carry the money to

Savannah or Charleston and send it by ship to Liverpool for the account of the Confederate government.[639] After making the $86,000 pay out, Clark had accounted for all except $53,977.10 of the gold and specie that he said left Danville. After President Davis met with his Confederate Cabinet for the last time on May 5, 1865, in Washington, Georgia, his plan was to go south far enough to pass points occupied by Federal troops and then turn to the west, cross the Chattahoochie, and meet the forces still supposed to be in the field in Alabama.

"If there should be no prospect of a successful resistance east of the Mississippi, I intended to cross to the Trans-Mississippi Department, where I believed Generals E. K. Smith and Magruder would continue to uphold our cause," Davis said.[640]

At Washington, Secretary of the Navy Mallory left Davis to move his family to safety.[641] And Davis, accompanied by ten men and five of his personal staff, prepared to leave Washington. Secretary Reagan remained for a short time to transfer to Mr. (James A.) Semple and Mr. (Edward M.) Tidball the treasure in his hands, except for a few thousand dollars.[642]

As Clark returned to his train to get some necessary articles, President Davis rode up with his party, and, after what Clark supposed were farewell words that passed between the President and others at the station, the train under charge of its quartermaster, moved out, while Davis headed southwest through Georgia with his military escort. [643]

"After leaving Washington I overtook a commissary and quartermaster's train, having public papers of value in charge, and finding that they had no experienced woodman with it, I gave them four of the men of my party, and went on with the rest," Davis said.[644] As the

President's party approached Sandersville, Georgia, on May 5, they heard disturbing reports from Mrs. Davis's entourage who were afraid that stragglers might attempt to steal their horses. The President decided next morning to take his staff and join her for a few days.

Although Davis decided to abandon "everything on wheels" near Sandersville, Clark remained with the train, even though the chances of capture were steadily increasing.

As Clark approached Sandersville, Georgia, he was halted by Major R. J. Moses and asked to turn over to him the specie that he said President Davis, before he left, had ordered to be placed at the disposal of the Commissary Department. Moses wanted to feed the paroled soldiers

Jefferson Davis said goodbye to his escort two days before his capture. Illustrated London News, July 22, 1865 *Source: Ernest F. Hollings Special Collection Library, University of South Carolina*

and stragglers passing through to prevent their burdening a section already stripped of supplies, so Clark turned over to Moses the wagons and silver bullion, and all of the escort except about ten men."[645] Clark said the payment to Major Moses was $40,000.[646] After reaching Sandersville, Georgia, Clark found the President and staff, and a few others, Captain Given Campbell and twelve of his men.[647]

"I inquired as to the funds of the staff, and found that they had only a small amount of paper currency each, except, perhaps, Colonel F. R. Lubbock, A.D.C, who had, I believe, a little specie of his private funds," Clark said. "Colonel William Preston Johnston told me that the President's purse contained paper money only."[648]

Clark said that they would need money for their supplies en route and to buy boats in Florida, etc., and he wanted to pay over to them funds to be used for those purposes, and they consented. So on May 5 near Sandersville, he paid, with Reagan's concurrence $1,500 in gold each to Colonel John Taylor Wood, A. D. C; Colonel William Preston Johnston, A. D. C.; Colonel F. R. Lubbock, A. D. C, and Colonel C. E. Thorburn (a naval purchasing agent who was with the party). Clark also paid to each $10 in silver for small uses, from a little executive office fund, which he had obtained in Danville, Virginia, "by converting my paper when the Treasurer was selling silver there," he said. "For this I took no receipt, charging it in my office accounts." He also gave Captain Given Campbell $300 in gold for himself and his men.[649]

Clark tried to give Reagan $3,500 in gold to carry in his saddle-bags as an additional fund in case of accidents or separation. "Reagan resisted, saying that he was already weighted by some $2,000 of his own personal funds, which he had brought out from Richmond, Virginia, in a belt around his person; but after some argument, he put the gold in his saddlebags and "'Good-by' was said," Davis said.[650] By that time, Clark had accounted for all of the $327,022.90 in treasury gold and specie that had left Danville except for $4,437.10.

Still trailing after Davis, Breckinridge continued trying to overtake the Presidential party, but he would turn to the east after he heard on May 10 of Davis' capture. On the way Breckinridge met J. Taylor Wood. They reached the Florida coast unmolested and, in an open boat, crossed the straits to the West Indies.[651]

As Davis and his small escort rode steadily south to catch up with his wife, he continued to be disappointed that, in his opinion, Johnston had surrendered unnecessarily in Durham. "The cavalry command left at the Savannah River was paroled, on the condition of returning home and remaining unmolested, and the troops inclined to accept those terms," Davis said.

"Had General Johnston obeyed the order sent to him from Charlotte, and moved on the route selected by himself, with all his cavalry, so much of the infantry as could be mounted, and the light artillery, he could not have been successfully pursued by General Sherman. His force, united to that I had assembled at Charlotte, would have been sufficient to vanquish any troops which the enemy had between us and the Mississippi River.[652] Had the cavalry with which I left Charlotte been associated with a force large enough to inspire hope for the future, instead of being discouraged by the surrender of their rear, it would probably have gone on, and, when united with the forces of (Dabney H.) Maury, (Nathan Bedford) Forrest, and (Richard) Taylor, in Alabama and Mississippi, have constituted an army large enough to attract stragglers, and revive the drooping spirits of the country.[653] "In the worst view of the case, it should have

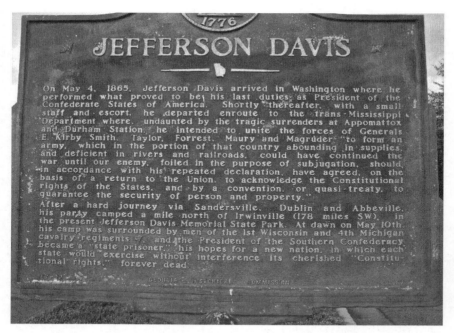

A marker in Washington, Georgia, describes the arrival of Jefferson Davis in the city on May 4, 1865, and his retreat through Sandersville and Dublin to Irwinville, Georgia, where he was captured on May 10. *Photo by Pat McNeely*

been able to cross to the Trans-Mississippi Department, and, there uniting with the armies of E. K. Smith and (John B.) Magruder, to form an army which, in the portion of that country abounding in supplies and deficient in rivers and railroads, could have continued the war until our enemy, foiled in the purpose of subjugation, should have agreed, on the basis of a return to the Union, to acknowledge the constitutional rights of the States, and by a convention, or quasi-treaty, to guarantee security of person and property. To this hope I clung, and if our independence could not be achieved, so much, at least, I trusted might be gained."[654]

22 THE CAPTURE OF PRESIDENT DAVIS

President Davis heard in Washington, Georgia, that his family had gone with his private secretary and seven paroled men who had offered their services as an escort to the Florida coast. However, soon after leaving Washington, Davis heard that a band of marauders, supposed to be stragglers and deserters from both armies, were pursuing his family, whom he had not seen since they left Richmond. "I immediately changed direction and rode rapidly east across the country to overtake them," Davis said.[655]

"About nightfall the horses of my escort gave out, but I pressed on with Secretary Reagan and my personal staff. It was a bright moonlight night; and just before day, as the moon was sinking below the tree tops, I met a party of men in the road, who answered my questions by saying they belonged to an Alabama regiment; that they were coming from a village not far off, on their way homeward. Upon inquiry being made, they told me they had passed an encampment of wagons, with women and children, and asked me if we belonged to that party. Upon being answered in the affirmative, they took their leave."[656]

After a short time, he arrived at his wife's camp and was hailed by a voice that he recognized as that of his private secretary, Burton N. Harrison, who told him that the marauders had been hanging around the camp. He and others were on post around it and were expecting an assault as soon as the moon went down.[657]

"A silly story had got abroad that it was a treasure train, and the *auri sacrafames* had probably instigated these marauders, as it subsequently stimulated General (James H.) Wilson to send out a large cavalry force to capture the same train," Davis said.

Davis was correct in his assessment, and Federal troops were less than four hours behind him following an indistinct trail through poor and barren pine woods that were almost uninhabited.

After hearing on April 29 that Johnston had surrendered to Sherman, Wilson was told that Davis, "under escort of a considerable force of cavalry, and with a large amount of treasure in wagons, was marching south from Charlotte, with the intention of going west of the Mississippi River."[658]

General James H. Wilson
Source: Library of Congress

Wilson immediately sent detachments deep into Georgia to occupy an almost continuous line from the Etowah River north of Atlanta to Tallahassee, Florida, with patrols throughout the country and small detachments at railroad stations in the rear of the line.[659]

The marauders did not attack that night, and Davis travelled with his family two or three days, when, believing that they were out of the region of marauders, he decided to leave their encampment at nightfall to execute his original purpose."[660]

Davis rode away during a rain storm on May 7, and since his horses were tired from non-stop riding, he made little progress. Mrs. Davis caught up with him that evening at the ferry across the Ocmulgee River near Abbeville, Georgia, where they found the president asleep on the floor of a deserted house. In spite of the thunderstorms, Davis told Harrison to keep the wagons moving through the night, and he and his men would catch up in the morning. Davis rejoined his wife's wagon train the next day at around noon on May 8, and they pressed on toward Irwinville, which they reached at about 5 p.m. that afternoon.[661]

They had traveled 190 miles southwest since leaving Washington, Georgia, when they made camp in the pine regions near Irwinville. The next morning — May 9 — horses were saddled and Davis was ready to start when one of his staff who had ridden into the neighboring village returned and told him that he had heard that a marauding party intended to attack the camp that night.[662]

"This decided me to wait long enough to see whether there was any truth in the rumor, which I supposed would be ascertained in a few hours," Davis said. Later that evening he lay down in his wife's tent with his horse still saddled and his pistols in the holsters.[663]

"I lay down fully dressed to rest," Davis said. "Nothing occurred to rouse me until just before dawn, when my coachman (Jim Jones), a free colored man who clung to our fortunes, came and told me there was firing over the branch, just behind our encampment. I stepped out of my wife's tent and saw some horsemen, whom I immediately recognized as cavalry, deploying around the encampment.[664]

"I turned back and told my wife these were not the expected marauders, but regular troopers. She implored me to leave her at once. I hesitated, from unwillingness to do so, and lost a few precious moments before yielding to her importunity.[665]

"My horse and arms were near the road on which I expected to leave, and down which the cavalry approached; it was therefore impracticable for me to reach them. As it was quite dark in the tent, I picked up what was supposed to be my "raglan," a waterproof light overcoat, without sleeves; it was subsequently found to be my wife's, so very like my own as to be mistaken for it; as I started, my wife thoughtfully threw over my head and shoulders a shawl."[666]

Davis had gone perhaps fifteen or twenty yards when a Federal trooper from Colonel Benjamin Pritchard's command galloped up and ordered him to halt and surrender, to which Davis gave a defiant answer and, dropping the shawl and raglan from his shoulders, advanced toward him.[667]

"He levelled his carbine at me, but I expected, if he fired, he would miss me, and my intention was in that event to put my hand under his foot, tumble him off on the other side, spring into his saddle, and attempt to escape," Davis said. "My wife, who had been watching, when she saw the soldier aim his carbine at me, ran forward and threw her arms around me. Success depended on instantaneous action, and recognizing that the opportunity had been lost, I turned back, and, the morning being damp and chilly, passed on to a fire beyond the tent."[668]

While the camp was being plundered, which Mrs. Davis said "was done with great celerity, there was a shriek dreadful to hear, and our servants told us it came from a poor creature who, in prying up the lid of a trunk with his loaded musket, shot off his own hand. Out of this trunk the hooped skirt was procured, which had never been worn but which they purported to have removed from Mr. Davis's person."[669] In the days to follow, newspapers would run descriptive accounts and jeering editorial cartoons that depicted Davis wearing women's clothing and a hoop skirt when he was captured.

The President said, "Many falsehoods have been

uttered in regard to my capture, which have been exposed in publications by persons there present—by Secretary Reagan, by the members of my personal staff, and by the colored coachman, Jim Jones, which must have been convincing to all who desired to know the truth. We were, when prisoners, subjected to petty pillage, as described in the publications referred to, and in others; and to annoyances such as military *gentlemen* never commit or permit."670

Mrs. Davis said, "No hooped skirt could have been worn on our journey, even by me, without great inconvenience, and I had none with me except the new one in the trunk.

"I have long since ceased to combat falsehood when it has been uttered and scattered broadcast, a much less distance than this one has been borne upon the wings of hate and vilification, and I now rest the case, though, could the tortures wantonly inflicted when he was a helpless prisoner have been averted from my husband by any disguise, I should gladly have tried to persuade him to assume it; and who shall say the stratagem would not have been legitimate?"

In a veiled reference to Lincoln's flight through Baltimore, she said, "I would have availed myself of a Scotch cap and cloak, or any other expedient to avert from him the awful consequences of his capture."671

Davis had with him at the time of the capture his wife and three of his children; her sister; Postmaster and acting Treasurer Reagan; and Colonels Johnston, Francis Lubbock, who had been the governor of Texas; and John Taylor Wood, volunteer aides; Burton N. Harrison, secretary, and (according to Parker) Robert Woodward Barnwell of South Carolina. Parker said all of these except

JEFF'S LAST SHIFT.

Newspapers were filled with variations on the popular theme that Jefferson Davis was wearing women's clothing when he was captured by Federal soldiers. In this cartoon, he is shown in a wooded setting wearing a bonnet and dress and wielding a Bowie knife as he is depicted as unsuccessfully trying to flee from three armed Federal soldiers. One soldier grabs Davis's arm, while the others point their weapons at him. A woman, possibly Davis's wife, raises her hands in alarm. The quotation at bottom, attributed to Mrs. Davis, reads: "The men had better not provoke the President as he might hurt some of 'em." *Source: Library of Congress*

Barnwell were captured.[672] "Having several small children, one of them an infant, I expressed a preference for the easier route by water, supposing then, as he seemed to do, that I was to go to Washington City," Davis said. "He manifested a courteous, obliging temper. My preference as to the route was accorded."[673]

Davis' personal secretary, Harrison, who had accompanied Mrs. Davis to Washington, Georgia, resolved to stay with Davis, but was not allowed to go with him in the carriage. "His fidelity was rewarded by a long and rigorous imprisonment," Davis said.[674]

Davis told Pritchard that some of the men with him were on parole, that they were riding their own horses — private property —and he hoped they would be permitted to retain them. Davis said he had a distinct recollection that Pritchard promised him it should be done, but he learned later that their horses were taken "and some who were on parole, such as Major Moran, Captain Moody, Lieutenant Hathaway, Midshipman Howell, and Private Messec, who had not violated their obligation of parole, but were voluntarily travelling with my family to protect them from marauders, were prisoners of war, and all incarcerated in disregard of the protection promised when they surrendered," Davis said.[675]

"When we had travelled back a day's drive, as we were about to get in the wagons, a man galloped into camp waving over his head a printed slip of paper," Mrs. Davis said. "One of our servants told us it was Mr. Johnson's proclamation of a reward for Mr. Davis's capture as the accessory to Mr. Lincoln's assassination. I was much shocked, but Mr. Davis was quite unconcerned, and said, 'The miserable scoundrel who issued that proclamation knew better than these men that it was false.[676] Of course, such an accusation must fail at once; it may, however, render these people willing to assassinate me here.'"[677]

There was a perceptible change in the manner of the soldiers from this time. "The jibes and insults heaped upon us as they passed by, notwithstanding Colonel

Pritchard's efforts to suppress the expression of their detestation, were hard to bear," Mrs. Davis said."[678]

Within a short distance of Macon they were halted and the soldiers drawn up in line on either side of the road. "Our children crept close to their father, especially little Maggie, who put her arms about him and held him tightly, while from time to time he comforted her with tender words from the psalms of David, which he repeated as calmly and cheerfully as if he were surrounded by friends," Mrs. Davis said.[679]

"It is needless to say that as the men stood at ease, they expressed in words unfit for women's ears all that malice could suggest. In about an hour, Colonel Pritchard returned, and with him came a brigade, who testified their belief in Mr. Davis's guilt in the same manner."[680]

At Augusta, the Davises were taken aboard a steamer where they were joined by Vice President Alexander Stephens, who had been arrested at his home "Liberty Hall" near Crawfordsville, Georgia. Also on the steamer were the Honorable Clement C. Clay, a former U.S Senator from Alabama who had been one of the agents in Canada; and General Joe Wheeler, and his adjutant, General John Perkins Ralls.[681]

"At Port Royal, we were transferred to a sea-going vessel, which instead of going to Washington, D.C., anchored at Hampton Roads, Virginia," said Davis, who was transferred to Fortress Monroe.[682] He was in chains in a cell at first, and his health deteriorated, but conditions improved and his family was allowed to visit. He was never charged with any crime or tried, but was not released until May 13, 1867, more than two years after his capture in the woods of south Georgia.

23 NO GOLD WAS FOUND ON JEFFERSON DAVIS

Word spread quickly through the country that President Davis had been captured on May 10 near Irwinville, Georgia. The rest of the President's party was captured a few days later, and after their release from prison, several of the party told Mrs. Davis that everyone was robbed of all they had, except Colonel F. R. Lubbock, who, after stout resistance and great risk, retained his money, upon which the party subsisted during their long imprisonment at Fort Delaware.[683]

Sherman, who was still angry about accusations that he had allowed Davis to buy his way through North Carolina with Confederate gold, would write in later years in his memoirs that "some of it was paid to (Davis') escort, when it disbanded at or near Washington, Georgia, and at the time of his capture he had a small parcel of gold and silver coin, not to exceed ten thousand dollars, which is now retained in the United States Treasury-vault at Washington, and shown to the curious.[684] The thirteen millions of treasure, with which Jeff. Davis was to corrupt our armies and buy his escape, dwindled down to the contents of a hand valise," Sherman said.[685]

Captain M. H. Clark, of Clarksville, Tennessee, who was acting treasurer at the time of the surrender, denied Sherman's claim that Davis had upwards of $10,000 in gold and silver coin or a hand valise containing gold, or, in fact, any gold or money at all when he was captured.[686]

"No gold was found on President Davis when captured for he had none," Clark said.[687] "Davis could only have received it through me, and I paid him none. The Treasury train was never with President Davis's party. They found it at Abbeville, S.C., rode away and left it there, and rode away

Instead of denying allegations by President Johnson's administration that he had accepted a bribe to let Davis escape through North Carolina, Sherman was "angry about the tone and substance" of the published bulletins.
Source: Library of Congress

from Washington, Ga., shortly after its arrival there, while it was being turned over to me."[688] Clark noted that the receipts quoted are of two classes — payments to troops and clerks for their own services. "But to officers of higher rank, like Generals Bragg and Breckinridge, or to members of the President's military family, they were for transmission to a

Colonel Micajah H. Clark, last acting Secretary of the Treasury, said President Davis had no gold or any money when he was captured on May 10. Source: Louisiana Research Collection, Tulane University

distance, to be afterward accounted for to the Treasury Department," he said.[689]

Colonel W. Preston Johnston, who was an aide to the President, wrote a letter from Baton Rouge, Louisiana, to General Joseph R. Davis on January 6, 1882. "I accompanied President Davis from Richmond till his capture." Johnston said. "At Greensborough, N. C, I accepted a loan of $100 in gold, pressed upon me by a friend, as I had only Confederate money. I used this to pay the expenses of our military family. The sum was not quite exhausted when we were captured, as our incidental expenses were small.[690]

"Having been an intimate of President Davis's house, as well as a member of his military family, I know that he came out of the war a poor man," Johnston said. "I knew that $20 or $30 were distributed to each soldier. I was told by someone at Washington to draw that amount, but was too much engaged to do so."[691]

After leaving Washington, when President Davis determined to part company with the wagon train, Major Van Benthuysen, who had charge of it, handed Johnston $1,200 to transport and took his receipt for it. "I regarded it as a trust to be employed, if necessary, in getting our party to the Trans-Mississippi Department," Johnston said.[692]

"I am of the opinion that our party received from Major Van Benthuysen some $5,000 or $6,000, but am not fully advised. This full sum of $1,200 was taken from my holsters by men of the Second Michigan Regiment when I was captured. I am quite sure that President Davis could not have carried much money about him, as he handed me his derringer to carry, being too feeble to endure its weight."[693]

24 THE BANK GOLD AND THE CHENAULT FAMILY

General Sherman was still fuming about the accusations by the Johnson administration that President Davis had bought his way through North Carolina with Confederate gold, but more efforts to humiliate Sherman were waiting when he arrived back in Raleigh on May 9.

Sherman found that General Jefferson Davis (no relation to the Confederate President) and the 14th Corps had been ordered to be reviewed by General Henry Halleck. "This I forbade," Sherman said. "All the army knew of the insult that had been made me by the Secretary of War and General Halleck, and watched me closely to see if I would tamely submit. During the 9th I made a full and complete report of all these events, from the last report made at Goldsboro up to date, and the next day received orders to continue the march to Alexandria, near Washington."[694]

Sherman crossed over to Washington, D.C., to meet with many friends—among them Grant and President Johnson. Both assured him that they had had nothing to do with the publication of Stanton's war bulletins. Sherman refused a reconciliation meeting with Stanton, "but, on the contrary, resolved to resent what I considered an insult, as publicly as it was made."[695]

Two weeks later on May 24, Sherman and Howard and all of Sherman's staff rode slowly down Pennsylvania Avenue followed by Logan and the 15th Corps. All on the stand arose and saluted, and Sherman left his horse with orderlies and went upon the stand where he found his wife and their 8-year-old son Tom and her father. "Passing them, I shook hands with the President, General Grant, and each member of the cabinet," he said. "As I approached Mr. Stanton, he offered me his hand, but I declined it publicly, and the fact was universally noticed."[696]

Sherman took his post on the left of the President and stood watching for 6 1/2 hours while his armies, the 14th, 15th, 17th and 20th Corps, passed in review. "Many good

people, up to that time, had looked upon our Western army as a sort of mob," he said, "but the world then saw, and recognized the fact, that it was an army in the proper sense, well organized, well commanded and disciplined; and there was no wonder that it had swept through the South like a tornado."[697] As Sherman was reviewing his troops, President

General Sherman watched with President Johnson and General Grant as his troops rode in review down Pennsylvania Avenue in Washington, D.C., on May 24. Source: Harper's Weekly, June 10, 1865. Source: Ernest F. Hollings Special Collections Library, University of South Carolina.

Davis was being delivered to the prison at Fortress Monroe, Virginia, on the tip of the peninsula below Hampton News. And in Washington, Georgia, bank officials were loading the Richmond bank money onto wagons to start the trip back to Abbeville, South Carolina. The wagons were disguised to look like apple vendors.

As the treasure wagons approached Lincolnton, Georgia, that evening, about 18 miles outside of

Washington, Georgia, the escort camped near the home of the Rev. Dionysius Chenault in Lincoln County, about 15 miles northeast of Washington.[698]

At nightfall, guerillas attacked the camp and tied up the bank officers. "It was reported that during the robbery, gold and silver coins flowed ankle deep in the wagons," Lincoln County author and educator Otis Ashmore wrote in the December 1918 Georgia Historical Quarterly.[699] "Men filled bags with the precious metal; they stuffed their pockets, and some tied their trousers at the ankles and filled them with as much money as they could make off with. Many of the raiders escaped with their booty, and some hid sacks of gold in the neighboring woods till it could be moved without danger."[700]

General Edward Porter Alexander wrote in the *Louisville Courier Journal* in 1881 that he "organized a company of boys armed with pistols" and accompanied by Judge (William M.) Reese and one of the bank cashiers went out to arrest the guerrillas who had about $80,000.[701] Before returning to Washington, he said they had recovered a total of $120,000, but he said that "another $250,000 to $300,000 had been left in possession of the outlaws, who hid it under clumps of trees for the time being, and no more of it was ever obtained from them."[702]

By the time the gold and silver had arrived under escort back in Washington, Georgia, and was deposited again in the vault of the old branch Bank of the State of Georgia, the total amount being reported had been reduced to $110,000. General James B. Steedman, the Federal officer with headquarters in Augusta, said he took possession of $110,000 in Richmond bank funds in August 1865, and a U.S. Treasury agent delivered it to Washington, D.C., to be placed in the U.S. Treasury.[703]

Alexander, writing in the *Atlanta Constitution* in October, 1883, said Federal General Edward A. Wild, "already notorious for his harsh conduct towards the citizens of Norfolk, came to Washington and took possession of the money and went to Danburg (Georgia) to endeavor to find more." Alexander said Wild was guilty of all the outrages attributed to him.[704]

"The first thing they did was to kill the house dog, 'Jeff Davis,'" said Mary Ann Chenault Shumate, who was 17 years old at the time. "We children were all standing in the window watching to see what was going on, when the dog ran out and barked at them, they all laughed and shouted, 'Kill Jeff Davis, Kill Jeff Davis!' Pa hollered and begged them not to kill his dog, but they shot the poor thing dead, and punched him through with their bayonets. They had learned the name even of the dog before they came out, and they made a great laughing and hoorahing when they shot him because they had killed Jeff Davis."[705]

The military party took Dionysius (or "Nish" as he was called) Chenault, who was a local Methodist minister, and John and Frank Chennault out into the woods and put them to the "most excruciating torture in order to force a confession from them," Mary Ann said.[706]

Dionysius was a very large man, weighing about 300 pounds, and Frank, who was 16 years old, weighed about 200 pounds. The men had their hands tied behind their backs and swung up by the thumbs until their feet were lifted from the ground.[707]

"Brother Frank was not quite 16, but very big for his age, he weighed 200 pounds, so it was awful on him," Mary Ann said. "Pa was forty years old, and never very strong, he fainted under the suffering so dead away that they got scared and thought they had killed him. He never got over it. Their thumbs were all as black as the chimney when they came back home, and their hands were so black and swelled up that it was a long time before they could use them. They were swung up three times and kept hanging by the watch, counting the minutes, leaving them up just as long as they could stand it without being killed. They said the pain was so great that after the first time they begged the Yankees to shoot them dead rather than suffer so again."[708]

The three men were kept out in the woods all day and all night.[709] But these and other tortures failed to force a confession. They were brought out of the woods and the Federals arrested Mary Ann; her uncle, the Reverend Chenault and his wife; Mary Ann's mother and father, Mr. and Mrs. John N. Chenault (brother of Dionysius); her 16-year-old brother, Frank, and some of the servants.[710]

They were taken to Washington and submitted to the "most humiliating treatment during an investigation" that ended with their complete vindication and release, Mary Ann said.[711] Before being put in the jail in Washington, Mary Ann and her mother and aunt were strip-searched. "We cried and tried to cover ourselves, but it was no use to make a fuss; it only made things worse," Mary Ann said.[712] [713]

The Chenaults hired attorneys who went to Augusta and got an order to have them released. General Wild was sent away by the Federals, and when the Chenaults went to court, the box of jewelry that Mary Ann and Parker said that Breckinridge had left at the home of Mrs. J. D. Moss was brought into the courtroom, and Mary Ann's mother was allowed to pick out her things from among them.

Mary Ann said that when Breckinridge and his staff had camped at the Moss house, Breckinridge was carrying a box of jewelry that had been contributed by the women of the South for the building of a gunboat. Parker had also remembered a large box of jewelry (the size of a five-gallon can) that he said the President and the cabinet left with a widow lady who lived near the pontoon bridge across the Savannah River. He, too, believed it to be filled with jewelry that had been contributed by patriotic Confederate ladies at the end of 1864.[714]

"When (Breckinridge) went off next morning, he left this box with Mrs. Moss to cake care of," Mary Ann said. "She kept it for several weeks, until the Yankees heard of it and came and got it, at the same time they imprisoned us. They took all our own silver and jewelry, too, pretending that we got it from this box. The next night when the bank train came along, the soldiers thought it was the rest of the Confederate treasury, and charged the train because they had as good right to it as anybody else, and they didn't want the Yankees to get hold of it.[715]

"Pa's money was given back to him too, but it took a sight more to pay counsel and other expenses, so after all, we were robbed by the Yankee government instead of our robbing anybody," she said. "Pa was so particular about keeping his family clear, that month afterwards, when he found that a cousin of ours had got hold of some of that money, and carried it off to the mountains, and hid it away safe, he persuaded him to bring it back to Washington and give it up."[716]

General James B. Steedman, commander of that district with headquarters at Augusta, Ga., said officers proceeded with $110,000 of the Richmond bank money from Washington to Augusta, arriving there on August 1.[717] A Federal Treasury agent took possession of the specie at the end of August and transported it to Washington D.C.[718]

25 THE EXECUTION OF THE CONSPIRATORS

Two days after President Davis was captured in Irwinville, Georgia, the assassination trial in Washington, D.C., began on May 12 and lasted for about seven weeks, with 366 witnesses testifying.

Louis Weichmann, who had been released from custody, was one of the key witnesses, and all of the defendants were found guilty on June 30. Lewis Powell, David Herold, Mary Surratt and George Atzerodt were sentenced to death by hanging; Dr. Samuel Mudd, Samuel Arnold, and Michael O'Laughlen were sentenced to life in prison. Edward Spangler was sentenced to six years.[719]

"The prisoners had been defended on their trial by able counsel and every effort had been made particularly

The conspirators were tried by a military court including standing left to right: Brig. Gen. Thomas M. Harris, Maj. Gen. Lew Wallace, Maj. Gen. August V. Kautz, and Henry L. Burnett. Seated left to right: Lt. Col. David R. Clendenin, Col. C.H. Tompkins, Brig. Gen. Albion P. Howe, Brig. Gen. James Ekin, Maj. Gen. David Hunter, Brig. Gen. Robert S. Foster, John A. Binham, and Brig. Gen. Joseph Holt. *Source: Library of Congress*

The ropes were adjusted before the conspirators were hanged.
Source: Library of Congress

in the case of Mrs. Surratt to prevent the execution," said Buckingham, who was the manager at Ford's Theater and an eyewitness on the night of the assassination. Buckingham said. "All applications for clemency were however refused. The execution was under the charge of Major General (Winfield Scott) Hancock and the gallows was erected under the direction of Captain (C.) Roth of General (John F.) Hartranft's staff by workmen from the arsenal," Buckingham said.[720]

It was erected in the south yard of the courtyard of Washington Arsenal (now Fort McNair) between the old shoe shop and the wall, and the platform was reached by fifteen steps on the east side, and uprights on the west side supported beams from which hung four strong hemp ropes over a six-foot drop.[721] The day—July 7—was intensely hot, and the few hundred people who gathered at the Old Arsenal Penitentiary to witness the execution stood under umbrellas to protect themselves from the

The conspirators were hanged on July 7, 1865. Source: Library of Congress

piercing rays of the sun. A sentinel in full uniform paced on the top of the wall to the west, and "up to the time of the falling of the drop, the eyes of those in waiting turned eagerly backward expecting that a reprieve would come in the case of Mrs. Surratt," Buckingham said.[722]

"When the criminals had been placed upon the platform, General (John) Hartranft advanced to the front and read in a clear voice the death warrants of the prisoners."[723]

After the last few words of religious consolation to the doomed ones, Fathers Barnardin F. Wiget and Jacob Walter administered the dying service of the Catholic Church to Mrs. Surratt, holding the cross to her lips. Atzerodt seemed to be muttering a prayer. The Reverend Dr. Abram D. Gillette, the Reverend Dr. Mark Olds and the Reverend Dr. John G. Butler made earnest prayers in behalf of each of the three men,

Payne (or Powell), Herold and Atzerodt, and then the arms, ankles, and knees of all were bound.[724]

"The white caps were drawn over their heads, the prop was knocked away, the drop fell and the four criminals hung quivering in the air," Buckingham said.[725]

The four other prisoners were taken to the Dry Tortugas off Key West, Florida, where O'Laughlin died in prison of yellow fever in 1867. Mudd, Arnold, and Spangler were pardoned in February 1869 by President Johnson. Spangler, who died in 1875, insisted for the rest of his life that he had no connection to the plot beyond being the man Booth asked to hold his horse.[726]

Surratt escaped to Italy but was brought back and tried, but escaped on a plea of the statute of limitation.

Corbett, who disobeyed orders and killed Booth in the barn that night, spent the rest of his life in an insane asylum.[727] Garrett, in whose barn Booth and Herold had hidden at the end, was never arrested and never charged.

And Jones, who had played the most significant role in their escape across the river to Virginia, was never charged or tried and lived out his life as a government employee raising ten children.

Even though President Davis and the secret agents who had been in Canada were captured and imprisoned. They were never charged with conspiracy in Lincoln's assassination and never tried.

None of them were ever implicated in Lincoln's assassination, and no evidence ever surfaced that showed that any of them were part of the conspiracy. And there is no record that any of the reward money offered by the Johnson administration for their capture was ever paid.

26 THE HUNT FOR GOLD IN THE SOUTH AND ENGLAND

Records about the gold, silver and bullion from the Confederate Treasury and Richmond banks that were on Captain Parker's treasure train have been analyzed for more than 150 years as if there had been no other civilian or government assets in the rest of the Confederacy or foreign countries.

Except for $16,987 of the $450,000 in Richmond bank money that was restored 28 years after the war ended, almost nothing was returned from the vast amounts of gold, cotton and other valuables looted and confiscated throughout the Confederacy by Federal soldiers during the war and by treasury agents and imposters working on commission after the war. And the stream of regulations and law suits unleashed after the war ensured that every piece of Confederate gold that could be located and any remaining cotton that could be converted to gold after the war would wind up in Federal pockets and the U.S. Treasury.

During his campaign though Georgia and the Carolinas, Sherman had ordered that foragers could not give receipts for lost or confiscated property, but could only provide written certificates of the facts, if they chose. So almost no restitution was forthcoming for the thousands of civilian homes, barns and other properties that were confiscated or burned and the gold and valuables pillaged during Federal campaigns through the Confederacy.

Only an occasional piece of gold or silver was ever returned to the civilians who were robbed as the Federal troops passed through the Confederate states. U.S. Lieutenant Thomas G. Myers from Boston was particular to point out that Sherman was participating in the division of treasure that was stolen during his campaign. "Gen. Sherman has silver and gold enough to start a bank," he wrote. "His share in gold watches and chains alone at Columbia was two hundred and seventy-five ($275), (which in today's dollars would be worth about $4,125),[728]....Since the terms of dividing the confiscated gold and jewelry was not an official written policy, he cautioned his wife not to show the letter out of the family.[729]

From time to time, someone reports finding Confederate gold. As recently as May 28, 2015, USA Today reported that treasure hunters followed directions to what they believe is $2 million in stolen Confederate gold in Lake Michigan. One of the treasure hunters, Frederick J. Monroe, said, "My grandfather told me a story that he heard from a lighthouse keeper, who originally heard it during a deathbed confession, that there's two million dollars of gold bullion inside a boxcar that fell off a ferry into Lake Michigan.'"[730]

After four years of research, Monroe and Kevin Dykstra discovered a sunken boat in January in the exact site in Lake Michigan that George Alexander Abbott said in his 1921 deathbed confession in Muskegon, Michigan. The pair of treasure hunters had begun scanning Lake Michigan off the coast of Frankfort as soon as the ice melted and found the boxcar described by Abbott that they believe holds more than $2 million in gold bullion.[731]

The state of Michigan can decide to send somebody to the wreck site to excavate the safe, or it can issue Dykstra and Monroe a permit to retrieve the safe themselves. Or it can decide that nothing is to be done, which means the safe and its contents will remain a mystery.[732]

Very little has resurfaced from the looting and pillaging throughout the Confederate states, including the Trans-Mississippi Department of General Smith, who had been selling cotton to Mexico at huge profits. Gold and money was known to be in the Confederate Treasury in

Shreveport, Louisiana, where Smith had his headquarters and that was operating as a separate entity when the war was coming to an end.

Most of the $450,000 in gold from the Richmond banks that left Washington, Georgia, on May 24, 1865, trickled away in a trail of robberies and rumors of scattered and buried gold that became so widespread that fortune hunters are still looking today.

The court records said that $450,000 in gold, silver and bullion was still in the bank in Washington, Georgia, when bank officials left on May 24, 1865. They reported $250,000 stolen at the Chenault place, of which $110,000 was recovered and returned to Washington, Georgia. However, $140,000 was never recovered, and there was no accounting for another $200,000 of the $450,000 that everybody agreed had left Washington, Georgia.

In the end, Federals seized the recovered $110,000, which was all that could be found of what was left of the recaptured bank gold that left Richmond on April 2, but no mention was made of the other $340,000 that was still missing when treasury agents left for Washington, D.C.

"A good many others, when they saw how things were going, got uneasy and gave up their share, and so the Yankees got a good deal of it, but there were oceans more of it scattered all over Wilkes and Lincoln counties, besides what was carried off," said Mary Ann Chenault Shumate, who survived the ordeal with her family.

"Some of it was hid about in swamps and woods, some was buried in the ground, and there is no telling how much has been forgotten and not found again," Shumate said.[733]

Rumors began to circulate that "bags of gold were hidden about in the woods by those of the raiders who

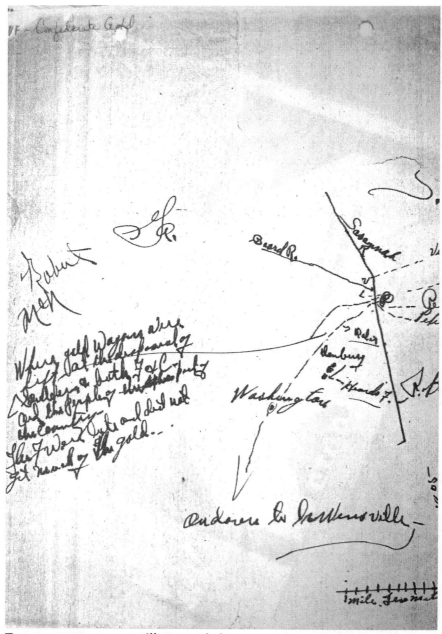

Treasure maps are still around that may show the way to buried Confederate gold. Source: Mary Willis Library, Washington, Georgia

could not get away with it at once, and there was considerable truth in those reports," Mary Ann said. "One of the prominent citizens of Lincoln County, who took no part in the raid, found about $10,000 in gold concealed near the scene and carried it home with him. For some time he said nothing about it, and no one suspected him. General Wilde had offered a reward of ten per cent of any of the funds that might be returned to him. Whereupon this gentleman took a portion of his find to Washington and claimed the offered reward. He was at once put to torture and made to surrender the whole amount without receiving any reward at all."[734]

For many years after the raid, rumors of hidden treasure continued to spread. "One of these twenty or thirty years after came from a statement said to have been made by a dying man in the West, who claimed that he was in the raid, and that he threw a large bag of gold into a certain part of Fishing Creek," Mary Ann said. "The particulars of his statement seemed so plausible that some parties undertook to pump out this part of the creek, which had in the meantime been cut off from the main stream and partly filled in. No treasure, however, was found."[735] [736]

Stories are still being told in the Carolinas and Georgia about all the gold and silver and other valuables that were stolen or disappeared during and after the Civil War[737] or were buried in wells, creeks, swamps, hollow trees, rocks, tree stumps and hidden inside walls of houses and barns.

One persistent legend is that Sylvester Mumford, a Confederate sympathizer who was supposed to have attended a cabinet meeting in Washington, Georgia, somehow left with some of the treasury funds. Although nobody mentions his presence at any of the cabinet meetings, his daughter Goertner "Gertrude" Mumford

The rumor is that gold was buried with Vice President Alexander Stephens' dog, Rio, under a huge monument. However, Rio actually died in 1863. Source: Library of Congress

Parkhurst, who died in New York in 1946 at the age of 99, is supposed to have said she was returning the balance of the Confederate treasury to Southern hands when she left bequests and scholarships to the children of Brantley County, Thornwell Orphanage in South Carolina, the Presbyterian Church headquartered in Louisville, Kentucky, and Georgia College, then known as Georgia State College for Women. No documents or official records have ever been found to connect Confederate gold to the endowment and scholarships.[738]

Another rumor is that treasure was buried at the confluence of the Apalachee and Oconee rivers, and some say that gold was divided among the locals.[739]

Missing gold was rumored to be hidden in Crawfordville, Georgia, at Liberty Hill, the home of Confederate Vice President Alexander Stephens.

The rumor is that gold was buried with his dog, Rio, who was supposed to have died about that time and been buried under a huge monument. Rio actually died in 1863, but he was buried under a mound of red clay, which left plenty of time for gold to be buried there before the thirty-six-foot monument to Stephens was erected at the site in 1893.[740]

Rumors are also whispered about gold in a secret place in the Robert Toombs house in Washington, Georgia.

And gold-seekers are still trying to get permission to dig in the cemetery in Danville, Virginia, where Parker said money was taken from the treasury before he left with the treasure train. Parker reported that some of the treasure was taken at Danville "*by authority*," but he never said how much.

The primary accounting for Confederate gold was a detailed report by the last acting treasurer Micajah H. Clark, who described the fate of $500,000 in gold, silver and specie in the Confederate Treasury that left Richmond. Clark accounted for almost all except for

Gold was rumored to be hidden in the Robert Toombs house in Washington, Georgia. Source: Library of Congress

$172,977.10 that did not leave Danville. Treasure hunters are certain that some of that Confederate gold and 39 kegs of Mexican silver are still buried in the cemetery established there in 1863 and are still trying to get permission to dig.[741]

General Joe Johnston called for an accounting of a missing $2.5 million, which may have been at one time at the mint in Dahlonega, Georgia. In an interview with Colonel Frank Burr, of the Philadelphia *Press*, Johnston expressed his doubt about the honesty of the President of the Confederate States and intimated that he had made away with over two millions of Confederate treasure.[742]

For his figures, he said he cited General P. G. T. Beauregard's estimate, and declined to read Burr's report of the conversation before it was sent to the *Press* because, he said, "that was not necessary; no man ought to make a statement to a journalist that he was not willing to stand by." Nevertheless he felt a profound confidence that what he said would not be made public.[743]

Johnston may have been talking about the money that had been stored in the Bank of Louisiana in Columbus because almost that exact amount—$2.3 million in gold and $216,000 in silver specie (coins)—had been moved after New Orleans fell to Union forces, since that added up to $2,516,000, but its fate is unknown.

After a public uproar about Johnston's charges concerning missing Confederate treasury specie, he issued a statement claiming that he did not know that he was being interviewed for a newspaper article when he made the charges, but he did not retract his questions and accusations about the missing Confederate money.

The questions about lost gold and President Davis' involvement became so insistent and widespread after the war that Micajah Clark, who was the last acting secretary of the treasury, published an account of the money on Parker's treasure train in the papers of the Southern Historical Society in an effort to dispel rumors that Davis took any money for himself and his family.

Although Clark was only accounting for that portion of the gold, silver and specie in the Treasury that left Danville on Parker's treasure train on April 6, Clark and numerous witnesses said that Davis had no money when he was captured and that he lived out his life in relative poverty.

No one accounted for $13 million in gold that Davis' servant Jim Jones said he took to Newberry, South Carolina. That was the same amount that General Henry Halleck and Secretary of War Stanton believed that Sherman had been part of a bribe to let Davis escape through North Carolina. Halleck said in a letter to Stanton on April 26 that the bankers in Richmond estimated that the specie "moving south from Goldsboro" was "estimated here at from six to thirteen million dollars."[744]

Captain Parker believed he was guarding only $450,000 in Richmond bank money (plus the $500,000 in the Richmond treasury) and never mentioned getting an additional $13 million in gold and English notes in Newberry, S.C., and although Sherman never denied the allegations, he was "outraged" that the Johnson administration would believe that his army could be bribed to let Davis escape through North Carolina.

A ten-pound silver Confederate seal hidden by Davis' servant was never found, nor was there any accounting for the gold and silver and other specie in banks that were pillaged and robbed, such as the banks in Columbia, South Carolina.

No one returned the $275,000 in gold and silver confiscated by Union General E. L. Molineux in Macon or the gold that his soldiers plundered from civilians. This total included at least $35,000 worth of coins and bullion that had been left for hungry Confederates returning home. Molineux also seized $188,000 from the assets of the Central Railroad Bank of Savannah that was never returned, and the federal government confiscated $500,000 in assets from the Bank of Tennessee and its branches in Augusta at the end of the war.[745]Some Confederate assets and gold were still held in Liverpool, England, by Fraser and Trenholm, the unofficial arm of the Confederate government that handled transactions of cotton sales and procurement of supplies, munitions and military equipment, including ships. Most financial dealings of the Confederate government in Europe had been handled by Trenholm's two companies: Fraser and Trenholm and John Fraser and Company in Liverpool, England.

Trenholm, who had been a senior partner in both companies in Liverpool, resigned from his business positions related to the Confederacy when he became Secretary of the Treasury on July 18, 1864, but associates had continued as the financial clearing house and the force behind the ships running the blockade to ply the trade between the Confederacy and Europe. Trenholm, who resigned as Secretary of the Treasury in April 1865, was one of the wealthiest men in the South before the war, and he became one of the most significant targets of the Federal government after the war, along with his partners and various business interests.[746]

Even before Davis was captured on May 10, the relentless Federal hunt for gold began expanding as the Federal government launched and revalidated a stream of war regulations and confiscatory measures designed to seize and impound gold and cotton and to impose taxes throughout the Confederacy.[747]

The U.S. government had passed an act on July 17, 1862, that authorized the confiscation and sale of Confederate property and had given the military extraordinary powers to confiscate and destroy Confederate property. The Federals were authorized to claim three classes of property: "(1) 'captured' property or anything seized by the army and navy; (2) "abandoned" property, the owner being in the Confederate service, no matter whether his family were present or not; and (3) 'confiscable' property, or that liable to seizure and sale under the Confiscation Act of July 17, 1862."[748]

Sherman had used those acts most effectively in his devastating war on civilian property in his campaign through Georgia and the Carolinas and the burning of Columbia, South Carolina.

The U.S. Supreme Court had ruled on March 12, 1863, that "disloyal" owners might become "loyal" by pardon and thus have all rights of property restored. "This was the effect of proclamations of the President (Lincoln). The restoration of the proceeds (then) became the absolute right of persons pardoned."[749]

Those acts were still in place at the end of the war, but President Johnson and the U.S. Treasurer were blocked when they tried to return confiscated civilian property in the South. In an opinion issued on July 5, 1865, the U.S. Attorney General ruled that cotton and other property seized by the agents or the army was *de facto* and *de jure* captured property and that neither the President nor the Secretary of the Treasury had the power to restore property to the former owners.[750]

The Attorney General said that "Congress took notice of the fact that capture of private property on land had been made and would continue to be made by the armies as a necessary and proper means of diminishing the wealth and thus reducing the powers of the insurgent rulers," and that after a seizure had been made, there could be no question of whether the usages of war were observed or violated, except through the courts.[751]

The President and the Secretary of the Treasury were warned that they had no discretion in the matter of returning civilian property.[752] According to the opinion of the U.S. law officers, "No one who submitted to the Confederate States, obeyed their laws, and contributed to support their government ought to recover under the statute" of March 12, 1863.[753]

In a dissenting opinion in a cotton case before the court, Mr. Justice Walbridge A. Field, said that both of the acts enacted by Congress required legal proceedings before the title of owners could be divested. Field said that no proceedings for condemnation and forfeiture had ever been instituted by the government and that the title of the claimants remains "as perfect as it did on the day the cotton was seized."[754]

The Congressional acts of 1862 and 1863 and decisions by Congress and the Supreme Court to continue to enforce them were interpreted as an invitation to confiscate gold, seize cotton and tax and foreclose property in the former Confederate states.

Armed with powers from Congress and a ruling by the U.S. Supreme Court, treasury agents and imposters collecting commissions surged through the former Confederate states in search of gold and cotton and any other property or commodity that could be taxed or confiscated and turned into gold. [755]

Civilians who owned even a bale of cotton were targeted by U.S. Treasury Agents and by imposters posing as Federal agents on commission. The Federal government wasted no time launching legal and political efforts to claim as much Confederate gold as could be extracted through confiscation and taxes.

United States army wagons, guarded by soldiers, went over the country day and night, gathering cotton for persons who pretended to be Treasury agents, according to *New York Times* correspondent Benjamin C. Truman.[756]

Truman, who had been President Johnson's staff officer and confidential secretary as well as a *Times* correspondent during the Civil War, spent eight months in the Southern states as a special Commission in Johnson's scheme of reconstruction and an additional two months in Florida and South Carolina trying to correct abuses of the Direct Tax Commissioners and reporting on the government's hunt for gold and assaults on private property.[757]

"All petty thievery went unnoticed when the Treasury agents began operations," Truman said.[758] "They harried the land worse than an army of bummers. There was no protection against one. He claimed all cotton and unless bribed seized it. Thousands of bales were taken to which

George A. Trenholm Courtesy of the South Caroliniana Library at the University of South Carolina, Columbia

the government had not a shadow of claim."[759]

In November 1865, Truman said that nearly all the Treasury agents in Alabama "had been filling their pockets with cotton money and that $2,000,000 were unaccounted for. One agent took 2,000 bales on a vessel and went to France."[760]

The greatest concentrated Federal treasure hunt after the war was aimed at Great Britain through lawsuits in which Trenholm was frequently mentioned. The claims against England had developed because of the Proclamation of Neutrality that Queen Victoria issued on May 21, 1861, which had conferred belligerent status on the Confederacy.[761]

Senator Charles Sumner from Massachusetts said that British intervention had caused the war to last twice as long and claimed that England owed the United States half the cost of the war. Sumner and some members of Congress even demanded that Britain cede Canada to the United States as part of the settlement, but Canadians resisted and the claims were dropped.[762] A disappointed Secretary of State William Seward, who had negotiated the purchase of Alaska, had hoped to add Canada to the United States as compensation for the role Great Britain had played in the War.[763]

As Federal treasury agents and imposters on commission hunted for anything left of value in the former Confederate states, stories proliferated about the gold and silver that disappeared during the last fleeting days of the Civil War.[764] The stories and rumors about oceans of gold scattered along the trail from Richmond to Irwinville, Georgia, and carried off to Northern states and abroad are still being whispered by treasure hunters and are occasionally repeated in the media with screaming headlines. Most of the lingering stories center on the treasure that left Richmond on April 2, and litigation over the ownership of the $110,000 that was seized in Washington, Georgia, and deposited in the U.S. Treasury would continue until June 22, 1893.

On May 13, 1867, Former President Davis posted a $100,000 bond for his appearance in the U.S. Court at Richmond and was released. He never appeared in court and in December 1868, a *nolle presequi* was entered in the case so that, at the age of 59, he regained his personal liberty. He was never charged with any crime and never sought nor received a pardon.[765] After being released from prison, Davis retired to Beauvoir, a home fronting on the Gulf of Mexico on the Mississippi shore where he spent the rest of his life writing his memoirs.[766]

As late as 1869 when Grant became president, as many as ten lawsuits seeking gold and property were still pending against former Confederates and England.[767] In one of the last government lawsuits, Trenholm's son, William, and his associates were ordered to pay the United States $150,000 in gold plus interest and 2,000 pounds for costs.[768]

The Federal gold grab in England raged until the two countries signed a treaty on May 24, 1871, and agreed to arbitration. The trial on September 14, 1872, drove the countries to the brink of another war, but ended when the International Tribunal awarded the United States $15.5 million, of which $3 million was because England had allowed construction of the Alexandra for the Confederates.[769] England's payment of $15.5 million would amount to $294,748,665 in 2015 dollars.[770]

The legal maneuvering over the Richmond bank gold lasted so long that former President Davis died in 1889 without knowing how it ended.[771] It would not be until June 22, 1893, after twenty-eight years in court, that the U.S. Court of Claims would declare that $78,276 of the remaining Richmond bank money was the property of the United States. The decree said that the banks were entitled to the "proportion of the recovered money equal to that of the funds that the banks never loaned to the state of Virginia for the Confederate government but that had also traveled to Georgia in April 1865."

Claimants on behalf of the by-then-defunct banks received back from the $450,000 that left Richmond on April 2 a final settlement of $16,987.88. The rest was claimed by the federal government.[772]

And in 1948, the Richmond treasure chest on display in the Mary Willis Library in Washington, Georgia, was finally opened by Alvin Downs, a locksmith from

One of the gold chests that was left in Washington, Georgia, is in the Mary Willis Library in Washington, Georgia. *Photo by Pat McNeely*

Atlanta, who spent one-and-a-half hours figuring out how to open the unique lock.[773] He described the chest as a "tamper-proof, burglar-proof iron safe" immune from all but the most expert hands. "The ornate lock case on the front of the chest was a dummy," he said. "The real lock was in the hole in the top, through which children would try to see what was inside." The hole had been camouflaged with a band of iron.[774]

"The key that fit this lock must have been nearly a foot long because the post inside is almost as big as my little finger," Downs said. "I never saw a key that big."

When the lock was finally opened, nothing was left inside the chest except a 1929 Federal nickel.[775]

INDEX

A

B

C

D

E

F

G

H

J

K

L

M

N

O

P

Palmer, William J., 127, 149, 150, 175
Parker, William H., 56, 60, 61, 66, 67, 68, 69, 72, 73, 74, 77, 79, 80, 83, 84, 85, 86, 87, 88, 89, 98, 143, 144, 145, 153, 154, 155, 156, 203, 215, 216, 221, 227, 229
Payne, Lewis, 22, 95, 96, 97, 105, 106, 107, 108, 169, 220
Petersburg, Virginia, 45, 46, 53, 54, 71, 76
Petersen, William A., 101, 104, 110, 113, 117
Pinkerton, Allan, 5
Port Tobacco, Maryland, 20, 21, 158, 160
Potomac, 17, 19, 21, 157, 161, 165, 166, 245
Pritchard, Benjamin, 202

Q

Quesenberry, Mrs. Nicholas (Elizabeth), 161

R

Raleigh, 29, 30, 36, 76, 119, 121, 122, 178, 211
Rathbone, Henry, 98, 99, 101, 102, 103, 104
Reagan, John, 56, 68, 199, 203
Richmond, Virginia, 30, 32, 35, 75, 146, 148, 178
Romeo, 24

S

Salem Crossroads, S.C., 87, 88
Salisbury, N.C., 76, 77, 79, 80, 82
Savannah River, 57, 144, 216
Savannah, Georgia, 28, 75, 147
Schofield, John, 29, 178
Seward, Frederick, 98, 107, 108, 116, 222
Seward, William H., 24, 95, 96, 97, 105, 106, 107, 108, 109, 110, 113, 115, 116, 118, 234
Sherman, William T., General, 25, 26, 27, 28, 29, 30, 31, 32, 33, 34, 35, 36, 37, 38, 45, 55, 56, 63, 64, 65, 66, 75, 76, 81, 82, 83, 84, 87, 93, 95, 117, 118, 119, 120, 121, 122, 130, 145, 146, 147, 148, 149, 150, 151, 152, 153, 155, 156, 157, 171, 172, 173, 174, 177, 178, 200, 207,211, 212, 221, 229, 231
Slocum, Henry, General, 28, 30, 31, 122
Smith, Kirby, Edmund, General, 74, 131, 132, 133, 137, 138, 139, 140, 141, 142, 143, 174, 222, 223
Soldiers Home, 6

T

U

V

W

ENDNOTES

[1] Harper's Weekly, March 9, 1861.

[2] Ibid.

[3] Ibid.

[4] Ward Hill Lamon, and Dorothy Lamon Teillard, Recollections of Abraham Lincoln, 1847-1865, (Dorothy Lamon Teillard, Washington, D.C.,1911) 268, 269. Lamon, chapter 2.

[5] Ibid.

[6] Ibid.

[7] Ibid.

[8] Ibid.

[9] Ibid.

[10] Ibid.

[11] Ibid.

[12] Ibid., 269.

[13] Commander of the Army of the Potomac.

[14] After the general's defeat at Chancellorsville, Virginia,

[15] Abraham Lincoln to Joseph Hooker, 8 May 1863, *CW*, 6:202-3. Lincoln to Joseph Hooker, May 8, 1863, *The Collected Works of Abraham Lincoln*, ed. Roy P. Basler (New Brunswick, N.J.: Rutgers University Press, 1953-55), vol. 6, 202-3.

[16] John William Headley, Confederate Operations in Canada and New York, Neale Publishing, New York, 1906), https://archive.org/details/confederateopera00headuoft), 173. Also, Encylopediavirginia.org.

[17] Headley, 173.

[18] Ibid., 176.

[19] *Ronald S. Coddington, The Plot to Kill Jeff Davis, The New York Times, March 8, 2014.* *http://opinionator.blogs.nytimes.com/2014/03/08/the-plot-to-kill-jeff-davis/?_r=0 Coddington's sources included*

Samuel T. Kingston military service record, National Archives and Records Administration; New York Monuments Commission, "Final Report on the Battlefield at Gettysburg"; John Dahlgren, "Memoir of Ulric Dahlgren"; Philadelphia Inquirer, March 4, 1864; Frank Moore, "The Rebellion Record: A Diary of American Events"; Richmond Whig, March 8, 1864; The New York Times, March 10, 1864; The War of the Rebellion: A Compilation of the Official Records of the Union and Confederate Armies; Anne E. Kingston pension record, National Archives and Records Administration.

[20] *Coddington. Also, Encyclopediavirginia.org.*

[21] *Coddington. Also,*
http://opinionator.blogs.nytimes.com/2014/03/08/the-plot-to-kill-jeff-davis/?_r=0

[22] Headley, 210.
https://archive.org/stream/confederateopera00headuoft#page/478/mode/2uphttp://www.civilwarsignals.org/pages/spy/confedsecret/confedsecret.html. "Large numbers of persons went to see it. It was in a pine box, clothed in Confederate shirt and pants, and shrouded in a Confederate blanket," *The Richmond Whig* reported on March 8, 1864.

[23] Headley, 210.

[24] Ibid., 361.The leader, Clement L. Vallandigham, who was a vigorous supporter of constitutional state rights, served jail time for writing against the Federal government in 1863. He was expelled to the Confederacy and later made his way to Canada where he met with Confederate agents to procure weapons and support, but the revolt, which was scheduled August 16, 1864, never materialized.

[25] Ibid.

[26] Ibid., 381. Captain John Yates Beall was later captured

as a spy and executed on February 24, 1865.

27 Ibid., 210 and 381

28 The Confederates were led by Lieutenant Bennett H. Young.

29 Headley, op. cit., 294-296.

30 During the middle of Act II, after Brutus and his co-conspirators decided to assassinate Julius Caesar, the capacity crowd of 2,000 at the Winter Garden Theater on Broadway was startled on November 25, 1864, by fire-bells coming from every direction. After conferring with the theater manager, Brutus, played by Edwin Thomas Booth, announced from the stage that a small fire had broken out at the adjacent Lafarge House Hotel, but had been extinguished. The benefit performance, which also starred his brothers, Junius Brutus Jr. as Cassius and John Wilkes as Marc Antony, had been mounted to raise money for a statue of Shakespeare in Central Park, and resumed without further interruption. Not until the final curtain when exiting theatergoers heard newsboys calling headlines like "Rebel Plot: Attempt to Burn City" did they learn about the drama unfolding outside.

31 Headley, 296.

32 Kevin Dykstra and Frederick J. Monroe have been searching for the long-lost bullion for a year. "My grandfather told me a story that he heard from a lighthouse keeper, who originally heard it during a deathbed confession, that there's two million dollars of gold bullion inside a boxcar that fell off a ferry into Lake Michigan,'" Monroe said. They claim they have stumbled upon a 19th Century tug boat off of Frankfort, Michigan, with the cabin doors still intact. There is also a safe on the vessel, and the pair believe there is something hidden inside, and are now trying to pry it open.

http://www.usatoday.com/story/news/nation/2015/05/28/treasure-hunters-find-shipwreck-in-lake-michigan/28044245/

[33] Ibid.

[34] Ibid. Also, http://www.nytimes.com/2014/11/25/nyregion/as-booth-brothers-held-forth-1864-confederate-plot-against-new-york-fizzled.html?_r=0.

[35] Headley, op. cit., 288.

[36] Ibid, 402.

[37] Ibid, 409.

[38] $289,855 or about $20,000 a year in 1865, http://www.davemanuel.com/inflation-calculator.php?theyear=1913&amountmoney=20000

[39] Carte de viste photographs carried by Booth at the time of his capture. Artifacts in the museum collection, National Park Service, Ford's Theatre National Historic Site, Washington, D.C. Library of Congress.

[40] John Edward Buckingham, Reminiscences and Souvenirs of the Assassination of Abraham Lincoln, (Washington: Press of R.H. Darby, 1894), 41.

[41] Ibid., 41, 57.

[42] George Alfred Townsend, The Life, Crime, and Capture of John Wilkes Booth, with a full sketch of the conspiracy of which he was leader, and the pursuit, trial and execution of his accomplices. (Google eBook: 1886) http://www.gutenberg.org/ebooks/6628), 41.

[43] Ibid., 41.

[44] Buckingham, 33, 34.

[45] E.B. Long with Barbara Long, The Civil War Day by Day, (New York: Da Capo Press, 1971), 677.

[46] Townsend, 41.

[47] Ibid.

48 Ibid., 42.

49 Ibid., Also, Finis L. Bates, The Escape and Suicide of John Wilkes Booth or the first true account of Lincoln's Assassination containing a complete confession by Booth many years after the crime, (Carlisle, Massachusetts: Applewood Books, 1907) (Originally published: Naperville, Ill., Atlanta, Memphis, Tennessee: J. L. Nichols & Company, 1907), 37. https://books.google.com/books?id=PX9RjixQc6kC&print sec=frontcover&dq=john+wilkes+booth's+nephew+and+g eorge+davis+in+the+civil+war&hl=en&sa=X&ved=0CDQQ 6AEwBGoVChMIr9n6nbG9xwIVhooNCh3WzgdH#v=onep age&q&f=falsehttps://books.google.com/books?id=PX9Rj ixQc6kC&printsec=frontcover&dq=john+wilkes+booth's+ nephew+and+george+davis+in+the+civil+war&hl=en&sa =X&ved=0CDQQ6AEwBGoVChMIr9n6nbG9xwIVhooNCh3 WzgdH#v=onepage&q&f=false.

50 Lamon, 275.

51 Ibid., 275.

52 Thomas A. Jones, J. Wilkes Booth: An Account of His Sojourn in Southern Maryland After the Assassination of Abraham Lincoln, His Passage Across the Potomac, and His Death in Virginia (Chicago: Laird & Lee, 1893), 24.

53 Townsend, op. cit., 825. "His house was on a bluff eighty to one hundred feet high, from which he could look up the Potomac to the west, across Mathias Point, and see at least seven miles of the river-way, while his view down the Potomac was fully nine miles," according to George Alfred Townsend, a reporter for the New York World. After the war began, great numbers of fugitives, including lawyers, business men, women, resigned army officers, suspected persons—even the agents of foreign bankers and of foreign countries, came to his house asking to be sent

across the Potomac. He was proud that not one letter or paper crossing the Potomac was lost while he was in charge during the war.

Jones may have crossed the Potomac as many as 100 times before he was arrested in October 1861 and served six months in the old Capitol jail. He was released in March 1862.

[54] Jones, 11, 23, 24.

[55] Buckingham, 39.

[56] Ibid., 39, 40.

[57] Ibid., 40.

[58] Ibid.

[59] Ibid.

[60] Buckingham, 41.

[61] Ibid.

[62] Ibid.

[63] Ibid.

[64] Robert Strong Sworn to and subscribed before me this 20th day of March 1876 James A. Tait seal. Notary Public Lamon, 272, 273.

[65] Buckingham, 41.

[66] Ibid.

[67] Ibid.

[68] Ibid., 51.

[69] Ibid.

[70] William T. Sherman, The Memoirs of W.T. Sherman, all volumes (St. Louis, Missouri, January, 1875: Acheron Press: September 27, 2012: Amazon Digital Services, Inc.), 12,364.

[71] Ibid.

[72] Ibid., 12,375.

[73] Ibid., 12,387.

[74] Fleming, op. cit., 286-287. Ho. Ex. Doc., No. 78, 38th

Congress, 1st Sess. (Chase)
https://play.google.com/books/reader?id=k59scrAh_LQC
&printsec=frontcover&output=reader&hl=en&pg=GBS.PA
291
[75] Ho. Repts. No. 784, 51st Cong., 1st Sess., and No. 1377;
52nd Cong., 1st Sess.
[76] Sherman, 12,410.
[77] Ibid., 12,382.
[78] Ibid., 12,410.
[79] Ibid., 12,405.
[80] Ibid.
[81] Ibid., 12,393.
[82] Ibid., 12,439.
[83] Ibid., 12,647.
[84] Ibid., 12,671.
[85] Ibid., 12, 486.
[86] Ibid., 12,531.
[87] Ibid., 12,706.
[88] Ibid., 12,762.
[89] Ibid.
[90] Ibid., 12,910.
[91] Ibid.
[92] Ibid, 12,922.
[93] Ibid.
[94] Ibid., 12,934.
[95] Ibid.
[96] Ibid., 12,946.
[97] Ibid.
[98] Ibid.
[99] Ibid., 12,957.
[100] Ward Hill Lamon, Recollections of Abraham Lincoln,
1847-1865 (Cambridge: The University Press, 1911), 248,
249.

[101] Lamon, 248, 249.

[102] Sherman, 12,957.

[103] Varina Howell Davis, Jefferson Davis: Ex-President of the Confederate States of America, A Memoir by his Wife, Volume 2, (New York: Belford Company Publishers, 1890), 575. http://www.perseus.tufts.edu/hopper/text?doc=Perseus%3Atext%3A2001.05.0038%3Achapter%3D80

[104] Samuel Emory Davis born July 30, 1852 and died June 13, 1854; Margaret Howell Davis born Feb. 25, 1855 and died July 18, 1909; Jefferson Davis Jr. born Jan. 16, 1857 and died Oct. 16, 1878; Joseph Evan Davis born April 18, 1859 and died April 30, 1864; William Howell Davis born Dec. 6, 1861 and died Oct. 16, 1872; Varina Anne Davis born June 27, 1864 and died Sept. 18, 1898.

[105] Davis, 575, 576.

[106] Davis, 576.

[107] Ibid.

[108] Ibid., 577.

[109] Ibid.

[110] Ibid.

[111] James Morris Morgan, Recollections of a Rebel Reefer, (Cambridge, Boston and New York: Houghton Mifflin Company, The Riverside Press, 1917), 228, 229., http://docsouth.unc.edu/fpn/morganjames/morgan.html University of North Carolina at Chapel Hill, 1999.

[112] Morgan, 230.

[113] Ibid.

[114] Davis, 577.

[115] Davis, 578.

[116] Morgan, 231

[117] Mary Norton Kratt, Charlotte: Spirit of the New South, (Winston-Salem, North Carolina: John F. Blair Publisher,

1992), 67.

[118] Morgan, 231.

[119] Davis, 579.

[120] Ibid.

[121] Ibid.

[122] John Brown Gordon, Reminiscences of the Civil War, (New York: Charles Scribner's Sons, 1904), 413.

[123] Gordon, 415.

[124] Ibid., 419.

[125] Ibid.

[126] Ibid., 422.

[127] Ibid., 416.

[128] Ibid., 417.

[129] Fitzhugh Lee was a nephew of General Robert E. Lee.

[130] Davis, 592.

[131] Ibid.

[132] Davis 591, 592.

[133] "to be free from war's alarms." Davis, 592.

[134] Ibid.

[135] Colonel Miller Owen; In Camp and Battle. Davis, 592.

[136] Ibid.

[137] Ibid.

[138] Ibid.

[139] Davis, 593.

[140] Ibid.

[141] Ibid.

[142] Ibid.

[143] Ibid., 594.

[144] Ibid., 594.

[145] Davis, 582.

[146] Ibid.

[147] Ibid.

[148] Ibid.

[149] http://www.styleweekly.com/richmond/confederate-executive-office-building/Content?oid=1477696.
[150] Newberry (S.C.) Herald and News, Tuesday, Oct. 28, 1913.
[151] Ibid.
[152] Ibid.
[153] Ibid.
[154] Sherman, 699-698.
[155] Richmond Dispatch, July 16, 1893. http://chroniclingamerica.loc.gov/lccn/sn85038614/1893-07-16/ed-1/seq-1/Parker's note said some of this article is transcribed with the kind permission of the Messrs. Scribner from my 'Recollections of a Naval Officer," Charles Scribner's Sons, New York, 1883.
[156] When the records reached Charlotte with Davis and his escort, they were stored in the county court house, and in 1872, the U.S. government bought the records for $75,000.[156]
[157] George H. Shirk, The Great Seal of the Confederacy. http://digital.library.okstate.edu/Chronicles/v030/v030p309.pdf, 309-311 The seal in the museum had been cast in England and is 3 5/8 inches in diameter and ¾ inches thick.[157] [157]
[158] http://www.southernagrarian.com/confederate-seal/
[159] This part was covered over when the Clark's Hill (now known as J. Strom Thurmond) dam was built between 1946 and 1954.Report of the Chief of Engineers U.S. Army By United States. Army. Corps of Engineers U.S. Government Printing Office, 1879, 752.
[160] http://www.southernagrarian.com/confederate-seal/ https://en.wikipedia.org/wiki/Great_Seal_of_the_Confederate_States_of_Americacustody of the Cox family of Hamilton, Bermuda.

[161] Newberry Herald and News, Tuesday, Oct. 28, 1913.

[162] Ibid.

[163] Davis, 586.

[164] Ibid.

[165] The Richmond Dispatch, July 16, 1893. Chronicling America.

[166] Ibid.

[167] Richmond Dispatch, (Richmond, Va.) July 16, 1893 Chronicling America: Historic Newspapers: http://chroniclingamerica.loc.gov/lccn/sn85038614/1893-07-16/ed-1/seq-1/
Parker's highest permanent rank, in all of the navies with which he served, was that of Lieutenant. While commanding the *Beaufort*, however, photographic evidence indicates Parker wore the insignia of a Commander and, while head of the Confederate Naval Academy, was referred to as a Captain. Thus, for practical purposes, Parker's highest rank on active duty was that of Captain.

[168] William Harwar Parker, Recollections of a Naval Officer, 1841-1865 (New York: Charles Scribner's' Sons, 1883), 350.

[169] Ethel Trenholm Seabrook Nepveux, George A. Trenholm: Financial Genius of the Confederacy: His Associates and His Ships that Ran the Blockade, (Anderson, S.C.: Electric City Printing Company, 1999), 157-252.

[170] http://www.georgiaencyclopedia.org/articles/history-archaeology/confederate-gold

[171] Original entry by Robert Scott Davis, Wallace State College, Hanceville, Alabama, Confederate Gold, (History and Archaeology, Civil War and Reconstruction, 1861-187708/03/2007 Last edited by NGE Staff on

01/10/2014.
http://www.georgiaencyclopedia.org/articles/history-
archaeology/confederate-gold
172 John G. Barrett, The Civil War in North Carolina
(Chapel Hill: The University of North Carolina Press,
1963), 12.
173 Mary Norton Kratt, Charlotte: Spirit of the New South,
(Winston-Salem, North Carolina: John F. Blair Publisher,
1992), 68.
174 Walter Edgar, South Carolina: A History, (Columbia:
University of South Carolina, 1998), 372.
175 William T. Sherman, The Memoirs of W.T. Sherman, all
volumes (St. Louis, Missouri, January, 1875: Acheron
Press: September 27, 2012: Amazon Digital Services, Inc.),
12,232-12,234.
176 James G. Gibbes, Who Burnt Columbia, (Newberry, S.C.:
Elbert H. Aull Company, 1902), 60, 61.
177

http://www.measuringworth.com/uscompare/relativeva
lue.php.
178 Jamieson was known as "The Father of The Citadel"
because of legislation he introduced to establish a military
school in Charleston.
179 Robert Scott Davis, Wallace State College, Hanceville,
Alabama, Confederate Gold, (History and Archaeology,
Civil War and Reconstruction, 1861-1877 08/03/2007
Last edited by NGE Staff on 01/10/2014
http://www.georgiaencyclopedia.org/users/rdavis-n-
599.
180 The Richmond Dispatch, July 16, 1893. Chronicling
America.
181 Ibid.
182 Ibid.

[183] Sherman, 699-701.

[184] Davis, 864.

[185] Ibid., 873, 874.

[186] William Harwar Parker Recollections of a Naval Officer, 1841-1865 (New York, Charles Scribners' Sons, 1883), 351.

[187] Richmond Dispatch, (Richmond, Va.) July 16, 1893 Chronicling America: Historic Newspapers: http://chroniclingamerica.loc.gov/lccn/sn85038614/1893-07-16/ed-1/seq-1/ Parker had been the superintendent of the Confederate States Naval Academy from 1863-1865. His highest permanent rank, in all of the navies with which he served, was that of Lieutenant. While commanding the *Beaufort*, however, photographic evidence indicates Parker wore the insignia of a Commander and, while head of the Confederate Naval Academy, was referred to as a Captain. Thus, for practical purposes, Parker's highest rank on active duty was that of Captain.

[188] Richmond Dispatch, July 16, 1893.

[189] Davis, 583.

[190] Richmond Dispatch, July 16, 1893.

[191] Davis, 584.

[192] Ibid.

[193] Davis, 596.

[194] Ibid.

[195] Ibid.

[196] Davis, 592.

[197] Ibid.

[198] Richmond Dispatch, July 16, 1893.

[199] Davis, 592.

[200] Richmond Dispatch, July 16, 1893.

[201] Gold had been discovered in North Carolina in 1799,

and mining was big business in the Charlotte area in the early part of the 19th century. By 1830, the city had a weekly newspaper, Miners' and Farmers' Journal, reporting gold-mine news, and coin production reached $10,163,660 from 1837 to 1861.[201]

[202] Parker, 354.

[203] Ibid.

[204] Richmond Dispatch, Sunday, July 16, 1893.

[205] Ibid.

[206] Historynewsnetwork. http://historynewsnetwork.org/article/49088- See more at: http://historynewsnetwork.org/article/49088#sthash.WrYwAIDl.dpufEstablished in 1863, the cemetery is located right beside the railroad tracks. Evidence suggests that the silver may still be there today, according to the Historynewsnetwork. http://historynewsnetwork.org/article/49088- See more at: http://historynewsnetwork.org/article/49088#sthash.WrYwAIDl.dpuf

[207] http://historynewsnetwork.org/article/49088- See more at: http://historynewsnetwork.org/article/49088#sthash.WrYwAIDl.dpuf

[208] https://archive.org/stream/generalkirbysmit00noll/generalkirbysmit00noll_djvu.txt

[209] See more at: http://historynewsnetwork.org/article/49088#sthash.WrYwAIDl.dpuf http://historynewsnetwork.org/article/49088

[210] Parker, 355.

[211] Sherman, Ibid., 12,807.

[212] Ibid., 12,545, 12,546.

[213] Ibid.

[214] Ibid.

[215] Ibid., 12,546.

[216] Ibid., 13,162.

[217] Ibid., 13,185.

[218] Parker, 355.

[219] Long, 673.

[220] Mason, 22.

[221] Ibid.

[222] Parker, 355.

[223] Richmond Dispatch, July 16, 1893. <http://chroniclingamerica.loc.gov/lccn/sn85038614/1893-07-16/ed1/seq-1/

[224] Parker, 355.

[225] Ibid., 355, 356.

[226] Ibid., 356.

[227] Richmond Dispatch, July 16, 1893.

[228] Davis, 614

[229] Ibid., 620.

[230] Ibid., 621,

[231] Ibid., 622.

[232] Ibid.

[233] Ibid.

[234] Ibid.

[235] Ibid.

[236] Ibid.

[237] Long, 677.

[238] Davis, 608.

[239] Ibid.

[240] Ibid.

[241] William Harwar Parker, Recollections of a Naval

Officer, 1841-1865 (New York: Charles Scribner's' Sons, 1883), 356.

[242] Ibid., 356.

[243] Ibid.

[244] Ibid.

[245] Parker, 356.

[246] Ibid.

[247] Ibid.

[248] Ibid., See also, Morgan, 234.

[249] Parker, 356.

[250] Richmond Dispatch, July 16, 1893.

[251] Morgan, 234.

[252] Davis, 611.

[253] Morgan, 234, Parker 356.

[254] Parker, 356.

[255] Davis, 611.

[256] Parker, 357.

[257] Ibid.

[258] Ibid.

[259] Ibid.

[260] Ibid.

[261] Parker, 357.

[262] Parker, 358.

[263] Parker, 357.

[264] Parker, 358.

[265] Davis, 611.

[266] Parker, 358.

[267] Ibid.

[268] Davis, 612.

[269] Ward Hill Lamon, Recollections of Abraham Lincoln 1847–1865, (Lincoln: University of Nebraska Press, 1999), 117, 118.

[270] Lamon, 118.

271 Ibid.

272 Ibid., 118, 119.

273 Ibid.

274 Ibid., 116-117.

275 Ibid.

276 Ibid.

277 Ibid.

278 Lamon, 118, also 116–117.

279 Ibid., 118, 119.

280 Ibid.

281 Ibid.

282 Lamon, 119, 120.

283 Ibid.

284 Sherman, Ibid., 12,823.

285 Buckingham, Ibid., 19.

286 Buckingham, 35.

287 Ibid.

288 sometimes spelled O'Laughlen.

289 Jones, 49.

290 Long, 675.

291 Buckingham, 43.

292 Ibid.

293 Ibid.

294 Ibid.

295 Ibid., 14.

296 Paul Martin, Lincoln's Missing Bodyguard: What happened to Officer John Parker, the man who chose the wrong night to leave his post at Ford's Theater (http://www.smithsonianmag.com/history/lincolns-missing-bodyguard-12932069/#TVtDisiZCAVQfkYr.99 Parker was reprimanded but never fired. Even after the assassination, Parker stayed on the police force until 1868 when he was fired for sleeping on duty and went back to

work as a carpenter. He died in 1890 and is buried in an unmarked grave in Glenwood Cemetery, Washington, D.C.

[297] Ibid.

[298] Buckingham, 75, 76.

[299] Ibid.

[300] Buckingham, 13.

[301] Ibid., 7-9.

[302] Ibid.

[303] Townsend wrote under the pseudonym "Gath," and his daily reports were published in a book in 1886.

[304] George Alfred Townsend, The Life, Crime, and Capture of John Wilkes Booth, with a full sketch of the conspiracy of which he was leader, and the pursuit, tril and execution of his accomplices. (Google eBook) 1886 http://www.gutenberg.org/ebooks/6628.

[305] Townsend, 10.

[306] Ibid.

[307] Ibid.

[308] Buckingham, 13.

[309] Ibid.

[310] Buckingham, 15.

[311] Ibid., 75, 76.

[312] Ibid.

[313] Townsend, 10.

[314] Ibid.

[315] Buckingham, 75, 76, 14.

[316] Ibid., 60.

[317] Ibid., 14.

[318] Ibid., 75, 76.

[319] HK Rathbone Subscribed and sworn before me this 17th day of April 1865 AB Olin Justice of the Supreme Court of the District of Columbia.

[320] Buckingham, 75, 76.

[321] Townsend, 11.

[322] Buckingham, 19.

[323] sometimes spelled O'Laughlen.

[324] Townsend, 42.

[325] Ibid., 10.

[326] It was a controversial raid from Canada by Confederate soldiers meant to rob banks in retaliation for the Union Army burning Southern cities and to force the Union Army to divert troops to defend their northern border. It took place in St. Albans, Vermont, on October 19, 1864.

[327] Townsend, 41.

[328] Ibid., 10. The building was formerly the old Washington Club house.

[329] Townsend, 10, 11.

[330] Ibid., 11.

[331] Ibid.

[332] Ibid.

[333] Buckingham, 19

[334] Ibid., 21

[335] Townsend, 10.

[336] Ibid.

[337] Ibid.

[338] Ibid., 11.

[339] Ibid.

[340] Ibid.

[341] Townsend, 12.

[342] Buckingham, 24.

[343] Ibid., 75, 76.

[344] Townsend, 11.

[345] General Halleck, Attorney General Speed, Postmaster General Dennison, Assistant Secretary of the Treasury M.B.Field, Judge Otto, General Meigs, and others visited the chamber at times and then retired.

346 Buckingham, 23

347 Ibid., 24.

348 Ibid.

349 Townsend, 11.

350 Howard H. Peckham, James Tanner's Account of Lincoln's Death, Abraham *Lincoln's Quarterly*, (Vol. 2, no. 4) Collection: Abraham Lincoln Association Serials, 176.
http://quod.lib.umich.edu/a/alajournals/0599998.0002.004/26?rgn=full+text;view=image
http://www.mrlincolnswhitehouse.org/inside.asp?ID=635&subjectID=4.

351 Peckham, 178.

352 Ibid. There "were Generals (Henry) Halleck, Meiggs [sic], (Christopher C.) Augur and others, - all of the Cabinet excepting Mr. (William H.) Seward - Chief Justice (Salmon P.) Chase, and Chief Justice Carter [sic] of the District of Columbia, Andrew Johnson and many other distinguished men."

353 Peckham, 178.

354 Ibid., 177-179.

355 Ibid., 179.

356 Ibid., 177-179.

357 Ibid., 179

358 Ibid., 177-179.

359 Ibid.

360 Ibid., 179.

361 Buckingham, 24.

362 Around the bedside at this time were Secretaries Stanton Welles Usher, Attorney General James Speed, Postmaster General William Dennison, Jr., Assistant Secretary of the Treasury M.B. Field, Assistant Secretary of the Interior General Henry Halleck, General Montgomery C. Meigs, Senator Charles Sumner, F.R. Andrews of New

York, General John Blair Smith Todd of Dacotah, private secretary John Hay, Governor Richard J. Oglesby of Illinois, General Elon J. Farnsworth, Mrs. and Miss Kenny, Miss Clara Harris, Captain Robert Lincoln, son of the President, and Drs. E.W. Abbott, R.K. Stone, C.D. Gatch, Neal Hall and Leiberman.

363 Townsend, 12.

364 Ibid.

365 Ibid.

366 Ibid.

367 Ibid. "The facts above had been collected by Mr. Jerome B. Stillion before my arrival In Washington. The arrangement of them is my own," Townsend said.

368 Sherman, 13,220.

369 Ibid.

370 Ibid., 13,244.

371 Ibid.

372 Ibid., 13,268.

373 Ibid., 13,361.

374 Ibid., 13,280.

375 Ibid., 13,543.

376 Lamon, 251, 252.

377 Ibid., 13,292.

378 Ibid., 13,511.

379 Ibid., 13,372.

380 Long, 679.

381 Long, 679.

382 Patricia G. McNeely, Sherman's Flame and Blame Campaign through Georgia and the Carolinas ... and the burning of Columbia (Columbia, S.C.: Pat McNeely, 2014), 195.

383Kratt, 65, 66. General P.G.T Beauregard established headquarters at the William Phifer house at 722 North Tryon

Street at Eleventh Street when he arrived in Charlotte in late March.

384 Mason, 26.

385 Ibid., 22.

386 Ibid., 28. Map Source: Library of Congress: Ilustration by C. A. Kraus, published by J. H. Bufford's Sons Lith., Boston, New York and Chicago, 1886.

387 Ibid., 33.

388 Ibid., 29.

389 Ibid., 27.

390 Ibid., 29.

391 Ibid., 28.

392 Ibid., 28.

393 Ibid.

394 Frank H. Mason, General Stoneman's Last Campaign and the Pursuit of Jefferson Davis by Frank H. Mason, late captain Twelfth Ohio Volunteer Cavalry, Sketches of War History, 1861-1865: Volume 3, edited by Robert Hunter, William Henry Chamberlin United States, 1890), 21. https://books.google.com/books?id=WtoSAAAAYAAJ&lpg =PA21&ots=WODnUm867b&dq=%22General%20Stonem an's%20last%20campaign%20and%20the%20pursuit%2 0of%20Jefferson%20Davis%22&pg=PA21#v=onepage&q =%22General%20Stoneman's%20last%20campaign%20 and%20the%20pursuit%20of%20Jefferson%20Davis%2 2&f=false.

395 Mason, 21.

396 Ibid., 33.

397 Ibid., 31, 33.

398 Kratt, 68.

399 Benson John Lossing, Major Moderwall in Civil War: 1868: Pictorial History of the Civil War, Vol. III, (Carlisle, Mass.: Applewood Books, August 9, 2010), 504.

400 Mason, 31.

401 Kratt, 68.

402 Ibid.

403 Davis, 625.

404 Ibid., 629.

405 Ibid., 625.

406 Long, 679.

407 Davis, 625.

408 Ibid.

409 Arthur Howard Noll, General Kirby Smith, (University Press at the University of the South, Sewanee, Tennessee, December 28, 1907), 225. https://archive.org/stream/generalkirbysmit00noll/generalkirbysmit00noll_djvu.txt. Statue of Edmund Kirby Smith was given to the National Statuary Hall Collection by Florida in 1922. http://www.aoc.gov/capitol-hill/national-statuary-hall-collection/edmund-kirby-smith https://archive.org/stream/generalkirbysmit00noll/generalkirbysmit00noll_djvu.txt Also, Marker for image[409]

410 Noll, 224.

411 Ibid., 253.

412 Built in 1848, the house was demolished in 1960. Shreveport Sesquicentennial Commission marker.

413 Noll, 226

414 Ibid., 226

415 Ibid., 227

416 Ibid., 228

417 Ibid., 228

418 Nepveux, 44-50.

419 Ibid., 44.

420 http://www.liverpoolmuseums.org.uk/maritime/archive

/displays/fraser-trenholm/ Also, see Nepveux, 43.

[421] Nepveux, 45.

[422] Ibid., 44.

[423] Ibid., 44.

[424]

http://www.liverpoolmuseums.org.uk/maritime/archive/displays/fraser-trenholm/ Also, Nepveux, 45.

[425] Nepveux, 45, 46.

[426] Noll 228.

[427] Ibid.

[428] Ibid.

[429] Ibid.

[430] Ibid.

[431] Noll, 251.

[432] Ibid.

[433] The diplomat mentioned in the correspondence was Mr. Rose.

[434] Ibid.

[435] Ibid.

[436] Noll, 252.

[437] Noll, 252.

[438] Ibid.

[439] Ibid.

[440] The diplomat was referred to only as "Rose."

[441] Noll, 252.

[442] Ibid.

[443] Noll, 253.

[444] Ibid..

[445] Noll, 254.

[446] Ibid.

[447] Ibid.

[448] Ibid.

[449] Noll, 254.

[450] Ibid., 255.
[451] Ibid., 258.
[452] Ibid.
[453] Ibid.
[454] Ibid.
[455] Ibid., 258. Also,
https://archive.org/stream/generalkirbysmit00noll/gene
ralkirbysmit00noll_djvu.txt
[456] Parker, 358.
[457] Richmond Dispatch, July 16, 1893.
[458] Parker, 358.
[459] Ibid.
[460] Parker, 359.
[461] Ibid.
[462] Ibid.
[463] Ibid.
[464] Ibid.
[465] Ibid.
[466] Richmond Dispatch, Sunday, July 16, 1893.
[467] Ibid.
[468] Ibid.
[469] Long, 678.
[470] Long, 682.
[471] Kratt, 67-69.
[472] Sherman, 13,556.
[473] Ibid.
[474] Ibid., 13,429.
[475] Ibid., 13,533.
[476] Ibid., 13,680.
[477] Ibid., 13,691.
[478] Ibid., 13,680.
[479] Ibid., 13,690.
[480] Ibid., 13,702.

481 Ibid.

482 Long, 680, 681.

483 Mason, 31.

484 Mason, 32.

485 Sherman, 13,591.

486 Ibid.

487 Ibid.

488 Ibid.

489 Ibid., 13,603.

490 Ibid.

491 Parker, 360. "I finally called upon him in company with General (James Barnet) Fry and Commodore William Wallace Hunter and found that they took the same view of the matter that I did," Parker said.

492 Ibid.

493 Ibid.

494 Ibid.

495 Ibid.

496 Parker, 361.

497 Ibid.. … where he met for the last time Commodore Josiah Tattnall. "He was not on duty at this time and during the few days I was in Augusta I was much with him. The Commodore preserved his cheerfulness."

498 Parker, 362.

499 Ibid.

500 Ibid.

501 Davis, 613.

502 Ibid.

503 Richmond Dispatch, Sunday, July 16, 1893.

504 The farm was located in the middle of modern-day U.S. Route 301, about two miles south of Port Royal, Virginia.

505 Additional images at
 http://rogerjnorton.com/Lincoln40.html.

506 Jones, 54.

507 Ibid.

508 One historian believes that Booth broke his leg in a riding accident as he fled. See, Michael W. Kauffman Kauffman, American Brutus: John Wilkes Booth and the Lincoln Assassination, (New York: Random House, 2004).

509 Jones, 54, 55.

510 Townsend, 47.

511 Jones, 55.

512 Buckingham, 71.

513 Jones, 61.

514 Ibid., 82.

515 Ibid.

516 Ibid.

517 Ibid., 93.

518 Townsend, 826.

519 Jones, 96.

520 Ibid., 99.

521 Ibid.

522 Ibid.

523 Ibid., 115.

524 Ibid., 111, 112, spelled Stewart by Townsend.

525 Ibid., 113.

526 Sometimes spelled Dougherty.

527 Buckingham, 25.

528 Ibid.

529 Townsend, 37.

530 Buckingham, 27.

531 Townsend, 37.

532 Ibid.

533 Ibid.

534 Finis L. Bates, The Escape and Suicide of John Wilkes Booth or the first true account of Lincoln's Assassination

containing a complete confession by Booth many years after the crime, (Carlisle, Massachusetts: Applewood Books, 1907) (Originally published: Naperville, Ill., Ataltan, Memphis, Tennessee: J. L. Nichols & Company, 1907), 155, 174, 177.
https://books.google.com/books?id=PX9RjixQc6kC&print
sec=frontcover&dq=john+wilkes+booth's+nephew+and+g
eorge+davis+in+the+civil+war&hl=en&sa=X&ved=0CDQQ
6AEwBGoVChMIr9n6nbG9xwIVhooNCh3WzgdH#v=onep
age&q&f=false

[535] Bates, 177.

[536] Ibid., 174.

[537] Bates, 174. Davis said that General Dana[537] said, "He (Booth) was buried near the old jail and a battery of artillery drawn over his grave to obliterate all trace of it."

[538] Buckingham, 27, Jones, 114.

[539] Jones, 114.

[540] Buckingham, 27.

[541] Bates, op. cit., Preface.
https://books.google.com/books?id=PX9RjixQc6kC&print
sec=frontcover&dq=john+wilkes+booth's+nephew+and+g
eorge+davis+in+the+civil+war&hl=en&sa=X&ved=0CDQQ
6AEwBGoVChMIr9n6nbG9xwIVhooNCh3WzgdH#v=onep
age&q&f=falsehttps://books.google.com/books?id=PX9Rj
ixQc6kC&printsec=frontcover&dq=john+wilkes+booth's+
nephew+and+george+davis+in+the+civil+war&hl=en&sa
=X&ved=0CDQQ6AEwBGoVChMIr9n6nbG9xwIVhooNCh3
WzgdH#v=onepage&q&f=false.

[542] Ibid.
https://books.google.com/books?id=PX9RjixQc6kC&print
sec=frontcover&dq=john+wilkes+booth's+nephew+and+g
eorge+davis+in+the+civil+war&hl=en&sa=X&ved=0CDQQ
6AEwBGoVChMIr9n6nbG9xwIVhooNCh3WzgdH#v=onep

age&q&f=false

543 Ibid., 8, 35.

544 Maintaining that Mrs. Surratt was innocent, Davis said the only reason he went to her boarding house (as Booth) in 1864 was to meet with John Surratt,544 who was at the time in the secret service of the Southern Confederacy as a spy, plying his service between Richmond, Virginia, Washington, D.C., New York City and Montreal, Canada. He said he had visited Canada and deposited about $20,000 in gold in a bank in Canada because of the "uncertainty of monetary conditions in the United States at that time."544 In the account, he didn't say whether he had visited the Secret agents in Canada, and the only spy he mentioned was Surratt.544

545 Bates, 42.

546 Ibid., 44.

547 Ibid.

548 Ibid., 45.

549 Edward Colimore, Booth Mystery must remain so – for now (The Philadelphia Inquirer, April 1, 2013) http://articles.philly.com/2013-04-01/news/38165545_1_john-wilkes-booth-edwin-booth-booth-family-members "Although the results might be intriguing, and the temptation to exploit emerging technologies is strong, the need to preserve these bones for future generations compels us to decline the destructive test," wrote Carol Robinson, the Army's congressional actions manager for the U.S. Army Medical Command, which oversees the museum.

"The three vertebrae that were removed during an 1865 autopsy, believed to be [of] John Wilkes Booth, are unique and DNA testing may or may not yield the information desired," said the letter to U.S. Rep. Chris Van Hollen (D.,

Md.), who helped submit the request.

The answer is "beyond disappointing. . . . I'm angry," said Joanne Hulme, a Booth family descendant who lives in Philadelphia's Kensington section. "I would like to know who's buried in the family plot" in Baltimore's Green Mount Cemetery, where the assassin is allegedly interred.

"This never ends," she said Friday. "I may take this to my grave, but I will take it kicking and screaming."

Hulme's family and others - including Maryland educator and historian Nate Orlowek - sought permission in 1995 to open the grave believed to be Booth's but were thwarted by a judge who concluded its location could not be conclusively determined. Some reports had placed it at an undisclosed site in the cemetery. See more at: http://articles.philly.com/2013-04 01/news/38165545_1_john-wilkes-booth-edwin-booth-booth-family-members#sthash.JljGf0qo.dpuf

[550] Buckingham, op. cit., 27, http://rogerjnorton.com/Lincoln83.html

[551] Jones, 122.

[552] Ibid., 123.

[553] Ibid., 125.

[554] Townsend, 832.

[555] Ibid.

[556] http://www.findagrave.com/cgi-bin/fg.cgi?page=gr&GRid=9188182.

[557] Ibid., 629.

[558] Davis, op. cit., 625.

[559] Ibid., 625.

[560] Ibid., 632.

[561] Ibid., 627.

[562] Ibid., 625.

[563] Ibid., 626.

564 Ibid., 625, 626.

565 Ulysses S. Grant, The Civil War Memoirs of Ulysses S. Grant (New York: Charles L. Webster & Co.), 295.

566 Long, op. cit., 681.

567 Nepveux, op. cit., 158. From Fort Mill, Trenholm and his wife went to Chester where they joined his partner Theodore Wagner. They traveled through Winnsboro and Newberry en route to Abbeville in May. By then, President and Mrs. Davis were in Georgia on their way to Irwinville, where they were captured. Morgan and the Trenholm daughters, along with their son William and his family, had stayed in Abbeville.

568 South Carolina Historical Marker Guide, (Columbia: S.C. Department of Archives and History, 1998), 239.

569 Ibid., 240-241. Marker 46-11. The house was razed in 1956.

570 Hwy. S.C. 49 business.

571 Sherman, 13,726.

572 Ibid.,15,262.

573 South Carolina Historical Marker Guide, op. cit., 232. Intersection of S.C. 49 and Road 22, 10 miles SW of Union.

574 http://www.sciway.net/sc-photos/laurens-county/joanna.html

575 South Carolina Historical Marker Guide Marker, op. cit., 140. Marker 30-1, intersection of S.C. 56 and Road 38, about 2.5 miles SW of Joanna, 140.

576 George Davis and Samuel Cooper. http://www.stoppingpoints.com/north-carolina/sights.cgi?marker=Jefferson+Davis&cnty=Mecklenburg Davis

577 Parker, 363.

578 Ibid.

579 Ibid.

[580] Ibid.

[581] Ibid.

[582] Ibid.

[583] Ibid.

[584] Ibid., 364.

[585] Ibid.

[586] Ibid.

[587] Ibid.

[588] Long, 685.

[589] Davis, 867.

[590] Richmond Dispatch, Sunday, July 16, 1893.

[591] Ibid.

[592] Ibid.

[593] Ibid.

[594] Parker, 365.

[595] Ibid.

[596] Ibid.

[597] Ibid.

[598] Parker, 366.

[599] Ibid.

[600] Ibid.

[601] Ibid.

[602] Ibid., 367.

[603] Ibid.

[604] Ibid.

[605] Ibid., 368,

[606] Ibid.

[607] Ibid.

[608] South Carolina Historical Marker Guide, op. cit., 3 (306 North Main Street, Abbeville) 1-7.

[609] Parker, 368.

[610] Ibid., 369.

[611] Michael Cotton, The Final Days, Williamson Co. Cavalry.

A history of Company F, 4th TN Cavalry Regiments, CSA. 1994), 226. Also, Washington (Georgia) County Library files.

612 Citation: Andrew Johnson: "Proclamation 131 - Rewards for the Arrest of Jefferson Davis and Others," May 2, 1865. Online by Gerhard Peters and John T. Woolley, *The American Presidency Project.* http://www.presidency.ucsb.edu/ws/?pid=72356

613 Townsend, 41.

614 Ibid.

615 Ibid.

616 Parker, 369.

"A few days after this a passing soldier told me General Johnston had surrendered and showed me his parole," Parker said. "I called together the few officers still with me and told them that as we were in General Johnston's command, we must accept the conditions and now after the four years war in which I certainly never desired to figure as a prisoner, I did wish to be captured so that I might obtain my parole. Without it, I did not like to set out upon my return to Virginia. We had several alarms that the Federals were coming and upon such occasions, the officers would assemble at my quarters where we would await our fate like the Roman senators, but they came not and finally hearing that a troop of cavalry was in Washington, Ga. I sent a Lieutenant there with a letter to the commanding officer explaining my condition and inclosing a list of my officers. He very kindly spared us the trip to Washington by sending us paroles only requiring the officer I had sent over to swear us in which he accordingly did. Our party now consisted of Captain Rochelle, Professor McGuire and wife, my wife and myself and being far away from home, we began to cast about for means to get back to Virginia."

616 Morgan, 231.

617 Davis, 868. Davis said May 4; Long, 685, said May 3.

618 Davis, 632.

619 Hobbes, 11.

620 Davis, 870.

621 Ibid., 870, 871 Also, Otis Ashmore, The Story of the Confederate Treasure, *The Georgia Historical Quarterly*, Vol. 2, No. 3 (Georgia Historical Society: SEPTEMBER, 1918), 119-138. Stable URL: http://www.jstor.org/stable/40575586.

622 Davis, 871.

623 Ibid.

624 Ibid.

625 Ibid. Also, Richmond Dispatch, July 16, 1893.

626 Michael Cotten, The Williamson County Cavalry: a History of Company F, Fourth TN Cavalry Regiment, CSA, 1994, 226. The Final Days, Williamson Co. Cavalry. A history of Company F, 4th TN Cavalry Regiments, CSA. (Goodlettsville, 1994 Washington County Library)

627 Hobbes, 11.

628 Ibid.

629 Sometimes spelled Wheless.

630 Parker, 369.

631 Davis, 633.

632 Eliza Frances Andrews, Journal of a Georgia Woman 1870-1872, edited with an introduction by Kittrell Rushing, (Chattanooga: University of Tennessee Press, 2002), 122.

633 Ibid., 868.

634 Captain Clark, Louisville Courier Journal, Jan.13, 1882.

635 Davis, 874.

636 Ibid.

[637] Ibid., 631.

[638] Ibid. 874.

[639] Nepveux, op. cit., 158.

[640] Davis, op. cit., 636.

[641] Ibid. 631.

[642] Ibid

[643] Ibid., 868.

[644] Ibid., 636.

[645] Ibid., 874.

[646] Ibid

[647] Ibid

[648] Ibid

[649] Ibid., 875.

[650] Ibid., 876.

[651] Ibid., 634.

[652] Ibid

[653] Ibid., 634, 635.

[654] Ibid

[655] Davis, 636.

[656] Ibid.

[657] Ibid., 637.

[658] Mason, 515.

[659] Ibid.

[660] Davis, 637.

[661] Ibid. Also, see:
http://emergingcivilwar.com/2015/05/09/the-capture-of-jefferson-davis/

[662] Ibid.

[663] Ibid., 638.

[664] Ibid.

[665] Ibid.

[666] Ibid.

[667] Ibid., 639.

[668] Ibid.

[669] Ibid., 641.

[670] Ibid., 639.

[671] Ibid., 641.

[672] Richmond Dispatch, July 16, 1893.

[673] Davis, 645.

[674] Ibid.

[675] Ibid.

[676] Ibid., 642.

[677] Ibid., 645.

[678] Ibid., 643.

[679] Ibid.

[680] Ibid.

[681] Ibid., 645.

[682] Ibid., 645, 646.

[683] Davis, 876.

[684] Ibid.

[685] Sherman, 13,702.

[686] Louisville Courier-Journal, January 13, 1882.

[687] Ibid.

[688] Davis, 876.

[689] Ibid., 877.

[690] Ibid., 880.

[691] Ibid.

[692] Ibid., 879.

[693] Ibid., 880.

[694] Sherman, 13,738.

[695] Ibid., 13,749.

[696] Ibid.,13,772.

[697] Ibid., 13,784.

[698] Otis Ashmore, The Story of the Virginia Banks Funds: A Dramatic Episode of the War Between the States, (the Georgia Historical Quarterly, Vol. 2, No. 4, December

1918), 171-197. Published by: Georgia Historical Society Stable URL: http://www.jstor.org/stable/40575593.

[699] Ibid, 178.

[700] Ibid., 173.

[701] Ibid, 174.

[702] Ibid., 175.

[703] General E.P. Alexander in the *Louisville Courier Journal* in 1881. Also see Hobbs, op. cit.

[704] Ibid, 181. Also, see http://www.jstor.org/stable/40575593?seq=24#page_scan_tab_contents, 181.

[705] Otis Ashmore, The Story of the Virginia Banks Funds: A Dramatic Episode of the War between the States, (Georgia Historical Quarterly, Vol. 2, No. 4, December 1918, 171-197). Mary Ann Chenault Shumate, The Torturing of the Chenault Family, (Georgia Historical Quarterly, 181 http://www.jstor.org/stable/40575593?seq=9#page_scan_tab_contents.

[706] Ashmore, quoting Chenault, 181.

[707] Ibid, 181.

[708] Ibid, 181.

[709] Ibid, 181 http://www.jstor.org/stable/40575593?seq=24#page_scan_tab_contents

[710] Chenault, 181.

[711] Ibid. Ashmore, 178.

[712] Ibid, 182.

[713] Ashmore, 178.

[714] Richmond Dispatch, July 16, 1893.

[715] Ibid, 180

[716] Ibid, 183.

[717] Ibid, 186.

[718] Ibid, 187.

http://www.jstor.org/stable/40575593?seq=24#page_sc
an_tab_contents
[719] Long, 694.
[720] Buckingham, 27.
[721] Ibid., 29
[722] Ibid., 29
[723] Ibid., 27, 29.
[724] Ibid.
[725] Ibid., 29.
[726] Long, 694.
[727] Buckingham, 72.
[728]

http://www.measuringworth.com/uscompare/relativeva
lue.php.
[729] James G. Gibbes, Who Burnt Columbia? (Newberry,
South Carolina: Elbert H. Aull Company, 1902), 60, 61.
[730] Brent Ashcroft, Shipwreck discovery may lead to Great
Lakes treasure (WZZM-TV, Grand Rapids-Kalamazoo-
Battle Creek, Mich., USAToday,:
http://www.usatoday.com/story/news/nation/2015/05
/28/treasure-hunters-find-shipwreck-in-lake-
michigan/28044245/
[731] Ibid.
[732] Ibid.
[733] Ashmore, Chenault, 183.
[734] Ibid., 185.
[735] Ibid., 184, 185.
[736] Ibid., 185. See also,
http://www.jstor.org/stable/40575593?seq=24#page_sc
an_tab_contents
[737] Robert Scott Davis, Wallace State College, Hanceville,
Alabama, Confederate Gold, (History and Archaeology,
Civil War and Reconstruction, 1861-1877 08/03/2007

Last edited by NGE Staff on 01/10/2014

738 http://www.rootsweb.ancestry.com/~gabrantl/confedgo ld2.html

739 http://www.kudcom.com/www/gold.html

740 Liberty Hall, the home of the illustrious Confederate Vice President, the Gagenweb Project, http://www.rootsweb.ancestry.com/~gatalia2/liberty.ht ml . ihttps://southernsentinel.wordpress.com/the-lost-confederate-treasure/ See also, 1948 article in the Atlanta Journal http://savannahnow.com/stories/072801/LOCtreasure.s html#.VanQDXi5fFI.

741 Richmond Dispatch, Sunday, July 16, 1893.

742 Davis, 849.

743 Ibid., 848.

744 Sherman, 699.

745 Original entry by Robert Scott Davis, Wallace State College, Hanceville, Alabama, Confederate G old, (History and Archaeology, Civil War and Reconstruction, 1861-187708/03/2007 Last edited by NGE Staff on 01/10/2014. http://www.georgiaencyclopedia.org/articles/history-archaeology/confederate-gold

746 Nepveux, 215, 216.

747 Claims against Great Britain, 41st Congress, 1869-1871 No. 1397, Senate Executive Document No. 11, Vol. 5. And No. 1398 Senate Executive Document No. 11, Vol. 5 http://memory.loc.gov/ammem/amlaw/lwsslink.htm Recognition of the Confederacy as a belligerent power Appendix No. II: Pamphlet Entitled "Hasty Recognition," by George Bemis, Esq., and an article on the same subject, by the same author, from the New York Times of March

16, 1868. Hasty Recognition of Rebel Belligerency, and our Right to Complain of it.
http://memory.loc.gov/cgibin/ampage?collId=llss&fileName=1300/1397/llss1397.db&recNum=53&itemLink=r?ammem/hlaw:@field(DOCID+@lit(ss13972))%23139700 45&linkText=1

[748] Fleming, op. cit., 286-287. Ho. Ex. Doc., No. 78, 38th Congress, 1st Sess. (Chase)
https://play.google.com/books/reader?id=k59scrAh_LQC&printsec=frontcover&output=reader&hl=en&pg=GBS.PA291

[749] Ho. Repts. No. 784, 51st Cong., 1st Sess., and No. 1377; 52nd Cong., 1st Sess.

[750] Fleming, op. cit., 286
https://supreme.justia.com/cases/federal/us/87/459/case.html#F1
Ho. Repts., No. 784, 51 Cong., 1st Sess., and No. 1377; 52d Cong., 1st Sess.

[751] Ibid.

[752] Ho. Ex. Doc., No. 114, 39th Cong., 1st Session.

[753] See Sen. Ex. Doc., No. 22, 40th Cong. 2d Sess. Also, Sprott v. United States 87 U.S. 459 (1874) Case U.S. Supreme Court Sprott v. United States, 87 U.S. 20 Wall. 459 459 (1874) Sprott v. United States 87 U.S. (20 Wall.) 459 Appeal from the Court of Claims.

[754] Justia, U.S. Supreme Court, *Hanauer v. Doane* in the 12th of Wallace and *Hanauer v. Woodruff*,
https://supreme.justia.com/cases/federal/us/87/459/case.html#F1

[755]
https://supreme.justia.com/cases/federal/us/87/459/case.html#F1

[756] These were general agents, supervising special agents,

assistant special agents, local special agents, agency aids, aids to the revenue, customs officers, and superintendents of freedmen. Rules and Regulations, July 29, 1864. Ho. Mis. Doc., No. 190, 44th Cong., 1st Sess. 2 Amended regulations, Sec. IV, March 30, 1865. Also, see 1 See Brewer, p. 375, and Garrett, p. 587.

[757] Truman, N.Y. Times Correspondent. Walter Lywood Fleming, 293.[757] http://query.nytimes.com/mem/archive-free/pdf?res=9507EEDB1439E233A25753C3A9619C946 796D6CF

[758] http://query.nytimes.com/mem/archive-free/pdf?res=9507EEDB1439E233A25753C3A9619C946 796D6CF

[759] Ibid.

[760] New York Times, Aug. 30 and Nov. 2, 1865. Also, see Walter Lynwood Fleming Civil War and Reconstruction in Alabama, 293.

[761] A Century of Lawmaking for a New Nation: U.S. Congressional Document and Debates, 1774-1875, U.S. Serial Set, Number 1397, 12-15. http://memory.loc.gov/cgi-bin/ampage?collId=llss&fileName=1300/1397/llss1397.db&recNum=56&itemLink=r?ammem/hlaw:@field(DOCID+@lit(ss13972))%2313970045&linkText=1Claims against England: http://memory.loc.gov/cgi-bin/ampage?collId=llss&fileName=1300/1397/llss1397.db&recNum=56&itemLink=r?ammem/hlaw:@field(DOCID+@lit(ss13972))%2313970045&linkText=1Nepvaux, 215, 216. Also, The dispatch from the U.S. government declaring a blockade on the Confederate states arrived four days before the British government issued the Proclamation, which conferred belligerent status on the Confederate States and allowed Confederates to use

England as a military base. If Lincoln's proclamation had arrived before the British proclamation of neutrality was signed, their act would have been interpreted differently.

762 Nepveux, 215, 216.

763 Nepveux, 212.

764 Robert Scott Davis, Wallace State College, Hanceville, Alabama, Confederate Gold, (History and Archaeology, Civil War and Reconstruction, 1861-1877. http://www.georgiaencyclopedia.org/articles/history-archaeology/confederate-gold 08/03/2007 Last edited by NGE Staff on 01/10/2014.

765 Ibid.

766 Headley, 459, 460.

767 Nepveux, 213.

768 Ibid.

769 Nepveux, 215, 216.

770 http://www.in2013dollars.com/1872-dollars-in-2015?amount=15500000

771 Ibid, 194

772 Robert Scott Davis, op. cit.

773 The Atlanta Journal Magazine, May 9, 1948. Also, see Robert Pavey, Mystery of Lost Treasure Endures, The Augusta Chronicle, July 16, 2001, http://old.chronicle.augusta.com/stories/2001/07/16/met_319056.shtml

774 Ibid.

775 Ibid.

Professor Emerita Pat McNeely taught writing and reporting in the University of South Carolina School of Journalism for 33 years. Before joining the faculty, she was a reporter and editor for *The Greenville News*, *The State* and *The Columbia Record*. She is also the author of "Eyewitnesses to General Sherman's Atrocities in the Civil War," "Sherman's Flame and Blame Campaign through Georgia and the Carolinas ... and the burning of Columbia;" "Hand-written Recipes and Memories from America's First Families;" "Fighting Words: A Media History of South Carolina;" "Palmetto Press: A History of South Carolina Newspapers" and co-author of "Knights of the Quill: Confederate Correspondents and their Civil War Reporting."

Made in the USA
Columbia, SC
08 June 2023

17687000R00161